FREE TO BE

Rev Don Bloch, Ph.D.

ARCHWAY
PUBLISHING

Archway Publishing books may be ordered through booksellers or by contacting:

Archway Publishing
1663 Liberty Drive
Bloomington, IN 47403
www.archwaypublishing.com
844-669-3957

Because of the dynamic nature of the Internet, any web addresses or
links contained in this book may have changed since publication and
may no longer be valid. The views expressed in this work are solely those
of the author and do not necessarily reflect the views of the publisher,
and the publisher hereby disclaims any responsibility for them.

Any people depicted in stock imagery provided by Getty Images are
models, and such images are being used for illustrative purposes only.
Certain stock imagery © Getty Images.

Scripture quotations are taken from the Holy Bible, New Living Translation,
copyright ©1996, 2004, 2015 by Tyndale House Foundation. Used by permission
of Tyndale House Publishers, Carol Stream, Illinois 60188. All rights reserved.

Credit to Nancy Jantz & Ansley Ward for front cover design

ISBN: 978-1-6657-1847-9 (sc)
ISBN: 978-1-6657-1846-2 (hc)
ISBN: 978-1-6657-1848-6 (e)

Library of Congress Control Number: 2022901802

Print information available on the last page.

Archway Publishing rev. date: 03/04/2022

Dedication

As you read this book that has the potential of changing your outlook on the life God has given you, you will quickly learn how the title came into being. You will also learn of the importance of "Freedom Fighters" on your journey. I have dedicated this book to one of my closest Freedom Fighters, my wife, Anne.

Anne received a diagnosis of Multiple Myeloma, a cancer of the blood, about a year ago. At first, it was labeled, MGUS, and then manifested into this next stage. Along with this, she had injured her leg and went through months of treatments at a wound care center. In the midst if this, we had moved into our new home, hung pictures and fell in love with our new church family at Southeast Christian Church in Prospect, KY. It is interesting that we had spent over 40 years ministering to others through healing prayers, laying on of hands, deliverances – and now this "fight" in our lives!

Like a re-run of the Biblical story of Job, there was more to come. Recently, she was diagnosed with the non-curable disease, Parkinson's Disease and has recently begun treatments for the symptoms. We continue to focus on God's Word, and especially James 5:11 which reads, *we give great honor to those who endure suffering. For instance, you know about Job, a man of great endurance. You can see how the Lord was kind to him at the end, for the Lord is full of tenderness and mercy.*

We see a reminder of her situation – and hope - every time Anne enters the room where blood is drawn for analysis. There is a sign painted on the wall which reads as follows: *Life isn't about waiting for the storm to pass ... It's about learning to DANCE IN THE RAIN.*

We both rejoice in our Sunday worship and praise, and receive spiritual support and God's unconditional love, as she continues to exude the love and joy of Jesus to all she meets! She is a powerful witness and inspiration to the love of God, and to get us through whatever the evil one tries to throw our way. As I frequently claim, "The Best is yet to come." And as my parents used to quote my words spoken when I first traveled outside the city of St. Louis, Mo. as a six-year-old on a school bus to visit a dairy farm, "It's a great, wide, beautiful, wonderful world, isn't it!"

Anne is a well-armed soldier and truly my Freedom Fighter. Keep on dancing, my beloved! We're doing the "jitterbugging" together!

Dedication

This book is dedicated to the thousands (my estimate) of prayer ministers who have gone through the School of Healing Prayer sponsored by Christian Healing Ministries, Inc., of Jacksonville, Florida (including my wife Anne and me) over these forty-plus years. This was the dream of its founders and our mentors, Francis and Judith MacNutt, as they both saw the fruition of their dream as being for the glory of God. All under the direction of God's Holy Spirit, this group of Christian believers has been on the front lines of witnessing captives being set free to be. Some may even carry the wounds of the spiritual battle they have been waging on God's behalf.

Forwards, "Free to Be"

I have known Don Bloch for 30 years. People are simply drawn to him by his gentle countenance and deep insight. His quiet, loving spirit and wisdom drawn from years of time in the Word and personal experience make Don someone you want to listen to very closely. I am fortunate that he has taken the time to write this book.

Ben Goldsmith, CRU (Campus Crusade for Christ) Director of Church Ministry, Jacksonville, FL. for 45 years

Proverbs 13:14

"The instruction of the wise is like a life-giving fountain; those who accept it avoid the snares of death."

When a person lives to be 92 and is still actively involved in sharing wisdom, that person is one to whom I want to listen. For almost 25 years I have known and worked with Don Bloch and his wife Anne. During those years, many of the ideas shared in his latest book, Free to Be were shared in conversations at meals and meetings. Reading them in this book, reminds me of just how blessed I have been to know the Bloch's and to have benefited from their Holy Spirit inspired Wisdom that has helped me to live in freedom that Jesus Christ offers to those who call Him as savior.

For me it's simple! Why wouldn't you want to know what Don has learned in over 90 years of life and with over fifty years of being a follower of Jesus?

Freedom looks good on you!

Gee Sprague

United Methodist Elder, Retired

Through my prison ministry, I met a man who was serving a life sentence in a maximum-security prison in Florida. He shared with me, perhaps the most profound words I have ever heard: "I deserve to be here for the crimes I committed, but also deserve to be free." He was simply saying that all of God's children can be free from the personal prisons in which they find themselves. Don's book shares with the reader how Jesus can and will set you free. With Godly wisdom and insight, Don shares truths that will set you "Free_to Be." I have also found this book to be useful in my prayer ministry. Thank you, Don, for helping me to open my eyes to the potholes and stumbling blocks people encounter on their journey into freedom. This is a must read for every freedom fighter in God's kingdom.

Greg Toole
prayer minister of Christian Healing Ministries, freedom fighter, friend and Brother in Christ.

By the time I became pastor at CrossRoad Church, I quickly learned from the grateful testimonies of many of our church members that the Bloch's' ministry of healing, teaching, prayer, and pastoral counseling had rescued countless marriages, reconciled parents with their estranged children, helped people find recovery from the bondage of addiction, and restored untold numbers of hurting people to wholeness. And in short order, my own life became one of these testimonies. I count myself blessed beyond measure to be included in the enormous company of people forever changed by their ministry. The ripple effects of God's grace at work in people's lives through Don and Anne will be fully revealed only by the light of eternity.

I am thrilled that in his nineties, Don has fulfilled a lifelong dream to publish this book, with more books to follow, of course! In part, my happiness results simply from the fact that a good friend has achieved such a remarkable accomplishment, but it is more than that, too; I am overjoyed that because of this wonderful book, many people will now have access to the wisdom and spiritual insights that have guided Don's life and work across several decades (and multiple continents) of helping people of all backgrounds find freedom and wholeness in Christ.

So many of us are searching for freedom from prisons of our own making. We become ensnared by all sorts of traps: guilt from yesterday's mistakes, anxiety about tomorrow's uncertainties, grief over what or whom we've lost, shame over disappointing others or ourselves, and all of the various addictions and compulsive behaviors that temporarily numb our pain, only to leave us exhausted, empty, and further enslaved.

In *Free to Be*, Don draws deeply on a lifetime of experiencing freedom in Christ to help the rest of us discover the "abundant life" Jesus describes in John 10:10. On every page, Don's heart of humility infuses his stories and observations with a profound kindness that will relate with every reader, saints and skeptics alike, no matter where you are on your spiritual journey. From the famous quotation often attributed to Sri Lankan pastor and hymn writer Daniel Thambyrajah Niles, in this book Don is "one beggar telling another beggar where to find bread."

Don describes his adventure of faith in Jesus as learning how to dance. I really love this, so much so that I have started thinking about my own spiritual journey in the same terms. Dancing can feel awkward, even uncomfortable...unless we are willing to free ourselves from worrying about what other people think! So, let's learn to dance with the reckless abandon and wild joy of children of God. Let's dance with Jesus.

You and I are free to be.

Kevin Griffin

Lead pastor, CrossRoad Church

Don has lead thousands in most of the states, Canada and U.K., to see themselves as God sees them … free to be who God created them to be. Free to communicate with God and free to live in His presence. Proverbs 2:6 – *For the Lord grants wisdom! From his mouth come knowledge and understanding.* This so describes my husband, Don. Rejoice! And enjoy the fact that you are free to be!

Anne Bloch, spouse

Contents

Preface

The Spirit of the sovereign Lord is upon me, for the Lord has anointed me to bring good news to the poor. He has sent me to comfort the broken hearted and to proclaim the captives will be released and prisoners will be freed [freed to be].
—Isaiah 61:1

When he came to the village of Nazareth, his boyhood home, he went as usual to the synagogue on the Sabbath and stood to read scriptures. The scroll of Isaiah the prophet was handed to him. He unrolled the scroll and found the place where it is written, "The Spirit of the Lord is upon me for he has anointed me to bring good news to the poor. He has sent me to proclaim that captives will be set free and the time of the Lord's favor has come." He rolled up the scroll, handed it back to the attendant, and sat down. All eyes in the synagogue looked at him intently. Them he spoke to them and said, "The scripture you just heard has been fulfilled this very day!"
—Luke 4:16

Jesus our Messiah has set the captives free to be! For a kid growing up with Old Testament readings in the Jewish temple, this was my connection for moving from the Old Testament into Jesus of the New Testament.

For the Lord is the Spirit, and wherever the Spirit of the Lord is, there is freedom!

—2 Corinthians 3:17

Chapter 1

The Beginning: Why and How

Free to be: what does it mean? God's call upon our lives is to live in freedom with Him and with our neighbors. Yes, there are many steps to this freedom—also many barriers for us to conquer in order to be totally set free to be the one God created us to be, free in Him! And yet, God's Word claims through the atoning sacrifice of his only Son, Jesus our Messiah, that we are free of our sinful nature. I believe it is true that we are all born with an addiction called sin. The Gospel of John claims that if we have the Son, we are free indeed!

Never, ever allow Satan to convince you that with this freedom you are open to do whatever feels good. With your newfound freedom comes responsibility to God and your neighbors.

As I begin this godly project, I am taken back to my early pilgrimage on earth—the many times when as a four- or five-year-old growing up in Saint Louis and sitting on my mom's lap, I would listen as she read to me from my favorite book, *My Book House*. How I longed for those famous words as she read to me, "Once upon a time."

Now I share with you my own "once upon a time."

In my conversion to receive Jesus as Lord and Savior of my life, God used a movie and a jigsaw puzzle! I was forty years old when Jesus, my Messiah, entered my life. I believe I spent forty years in the desert just like my Hebrew relatives. I had just attended a weekend seminar at a local church in Louisville, Kentucky. This was sponsored by the Ecumenical Institute from Chicago, Illinois, and it attempted to correlate events that took place two thousand years ago with life today.

On May 11, 1969, at nine o'clock, *Zorba the Greek* was the Sunday night movie of the week. As I sat watching this movie unfold, I was worn out, exhausted, and confused about the weekend seminar I had just completed. It all reminded me of a difficult jigsaw puzzle.

You see, once upon a time, when I was a young lad growing up in the Depression, my family used jigsaw puzzles as a means of family entertainment in the evenings. I have always enjoyed—and perhaps been addicted to—such puzzles. As I was watching this movie, God was using my imagination and my love of jigsaw puzzles to zap me. In my imagination, I saw a puzzle on my lap. In the beginning of the movie, very few pieces fell into place, and as the movie progressed, they became easier to insert into the forming picture. The last line in the movie is the changed Englishman asking Zorba, "Teach me to dance." In other words, this is a request to embrace life in spite of the chaotic conditions in which we find ourselves and to be taught to embrace freedom and release our chains of bondage.

The exact second the movie ended, I put the last piece into the puzzle. What I saw was the smiling face of Jesus in the puzzle looking at me with such warmth and compassion as if to say, "I have been waiting for you. Come now and journey with Me." Thus, my journey into freedom began.

At that instant, God seemed to be telling me that God the Father *created* me to dance; God the Son gave me *permission* to dance; and God the Holy Spirit *taught* me to dance.

I believe these three things are the road signs on our journey into freedom. This journey can only begin when we know the statement of truth—who God is and who we are in relationship to and with God.

The first step of this journey into freedom comes with a decision made by both our heads and our hearts. It is not merely a head decision, because a decision of the heart is also required. We cannot rely only on the feelings from our heart. Making the decision involves a thoughtful confession to God that you seek Him and desire to walk into freedom with Him!

Let's look back to God the Holy Spirit teaching us to "dance." Consider this the "two-step." Step one: Begin the journey into freedom by making the decision as mentioned earlier. Step two: Walk into freedom, an ongoing process.

We cannot walk *in* freedom until we decide to walk *into* freedom! In my estimation, we have at least two requirements. We may as well tell ourselves at the beginning that we cannot do this by ourselves. God's plan or method of operation calls for *true* Christian fellowship. Note the italics. There are many deceivers along the pathway, and we will need discernment to protect us from these obstacles. I refer you to the classic book *Pilgrim's Progress*. Just relate your journey to the main character's journey in this book. You will find the following:

1. We need Christian colleagues not only to affirm us on our journey, but also to keep us accountable along the way. Some of us have grown up without this affirmation. This deprivation has harmed us. This lack, too, can be overcome with God. We still need our cheerleaders today. The body of Christ needs to pick up this task.

2. The other requirement along this journey into freedom is to be yoked with Jesus Christ. This means walking so close with Him that if Jesus is on our left side and makes a right turn, He bumps into us. We need to be that close!

There will be potholes—some quite deep—along the road. There will be forks in the road and a time of decision on our part as to which fork to take. Here, I share the famous New York Yankees coach Yogi Berra's famous quote, "When you come to a fork in the road, take it!" (More on stumbling blocks later.) There are also places along the road where Jesus will call us just to rest with Him—a God-given rest stop.

Speaking of potholes, some quotations from the book *Child Within* by Portia Nelson (1980) quite appropriately need to be shared at this time:

Autobiography in Five Short Chapters

1. I walk down the street. There is a deep hole in the sidewalk. I fall in. I am lost … I am hopeless. It isn't my fault. It takes forever to find a way out.

2. I walk down the same street. There is a deep hole in the sidewalk. I pretend I don't see it. I fall in again. I can't believe I am in the same place. But it isn't my fault. It still takes a long time to get out.

3. I walk down the same street. There is a deep hole in the sidewalk. I see it is there. I still fall in. … It's a habit. My eyes are open and I know where I am. It is *my* fault. I get out immediately.

4. I walk down the same street. There is a deep hole in the sidewalk. I walk around it.

5. I walk down a different street.

This recalls a vision God gave me a few years ago. Jesus and I were climbing a mountain together. We were obviously getting quite high up as I was not only worn out, but also worn down! I kept looking at the huge size of the mountain in front of me. Jesus noticed a tree along the way and suggested the two of us just relax and sit under it. Instead of looking from the side of the tree facing the mountain, we leaned back against the side of the tree facing the meadow and valley below. The sun was bouncing off the beautiful meadow wildflowers, and the gentle breeze blowing against my face was also blowing a few white fluffy cumulus clouds into the scene. Jesus was calling me to a rest—my own personal Sabbath rest! He was showing me not the task in front of me, but how far the two of us had traveled up the mountain together.

When God created this world, He also created a day of rest for us, and the first of His holidays that He gave us to celebrate is the Sabbath! Remember that such words as *relax, enjoy,* and *rejoice* are in God's vocabulary. Jesus calls us to be yoked with Him—to walk with Him. He is also asking us not to get out in front of Him, nor to lag behind. Our journey will be a continuing process, like walking in holiness. It is consummated when we walk into our permanent heavenly Jerusalem. In our effort to embrace this journey, we may find we have excess baggage that is weighing us down. *Free to Be* will address some of these issues and hopefully suggest how to lighten the load. Our journey into freedom has now begun! Praise the Lord!

Why "Free to Be"?

> So if the Son sets you free, you will be free indeed.
> —John 8:36

We come to know God as we attempt to know the Trinity. We need to learn, however, that the Trinity is part of the mystery of God, which we will not really understand, at least not on this side of heaven. As to the "Why free to be?" I need to sketch a few diagrams or triangles to attempt to explain. If I could draw an analogy of the Trinity of God, it would look something like this:

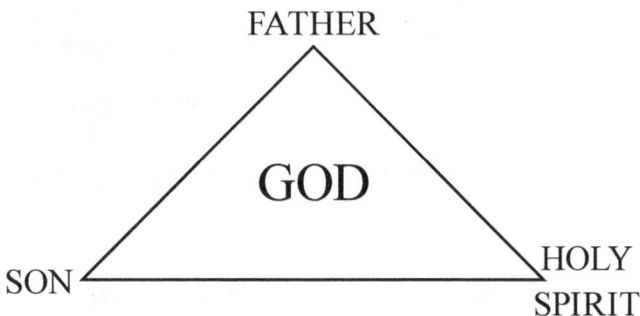

There are three parts to God's attributes too, the same three parts of the human character that make us who we are. These also could be classified as parts of our function as human beings. They are as follows:

```
              KNOWING
                 △
                / \
               /   \
              /     \
             /  GOD  \
            /         \
           /           \
   BEING  △─────────────△  DOING
```

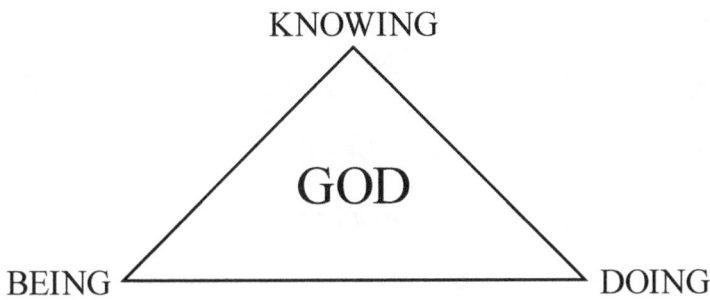

It is through the Father that we know who we are. It is through our being that we come to know Jesus, and it is through the power of the Holy Spirit that doing (action) takes place.

It is through the Father that we are free to know. It is through the Son that we are free to be. It is through the Holy Spirit that we are free to do.

Many of us receive freedom as we read God's Word and become liberated through this knowing. Many of us receive freedom as we carry out God's Word and work here on earth. However, many of us are bogged down and remain in bondage when it comes to *being* free in God's Word. We will discuss some of these bondages later in this writing.

I received a testimony from a Christian friend in South Carolina whom my wife and I had counseled. She had been set free from some of the things that had kept her in bondage.

When she learned of my desire to write on this topic, her comment was, "Amid all the fast-moving stuff, God continues his marvelous healing in my life, little by little, at His pace. I am truly transformed from years ago, and His mercies are new every morning. I love the concept of your proposed [book] title, *Free to Be*, since learning to *be* instead of *doing* all the time has been so central in my journey to wholeness."

As human beings, we tend to get wrapped up in knowing by undertaking much study and reading. This is not to be construed as bad, but it could be harmful if it is the *only* avenue. Likewise, we have a tendency to get so wrapped up in what we do that we lose sight of the study. Of course, we cannot neglect the thought of *Who am I?* As expected, we need to maintain a proper balance in all three of these areas of our lives as we journey into wholeness.

I recall an event in the life of a church when a church member dropped in to visit her pastor at his church office. She saw him sitting at his desk reading as she entered into the secretary's office. Since she had no appointment, he suggested she wait a few moments until he completed the thought he was pondering. The visitor became irate that her pastor just sat at his desk and studied when he could be *doing*! We all need study (to know); we all need to be; we all need to do. God tells us in James that faith without action is dead ("In the same way, faith by itself, if not accompanied by action, is dead" [James 2:17]).

God has called each of us to freedom. He has called us free to be that person He created us to be, a person whose life resonates with "love, joy, peace, forbearance, kindness, goodness, faithfulness, gentleness and self-control," as expressed in Galatians 5:22–23. I believe this freedom comes only through our relationship with Christ Jesus and from no other source!

God has called us into balance with Him. Let us be free to know, free to do, and free to be. As the author Josh McDowell has stated, "Remember that you are free to be the divine original that God created you to be. Enjoy your freedom and use it as an opportunity to grow and become more like Christ, expressing more and more the image of God."

Luke 10:38–42 tells us the story of two sisters, Mary and Martha, who have an encounter with Jesus. It is apparent that Mary is focusing on "being" in this situation as she desires to soak up as much as she possibly can by being at the feet of

Jesus. Martha even complains to her guest that it is unfair she is stuck with the "doing" and that her sister offered no help! To me, it appears that Mary is choosing to worship, and her sister is choosing to do rather than to be in order to impress her guest. I believe Jesus has a love for both Mary and Martha; however, He lovingly rebukes Martha after she makes a plea that He chastise Mary for not helping in the kitchen. It is important to remember that Jesus is on His way to Jerusalem and knows what awaits Him there. I doubt He is interested in what's for dinner.

We need to discern what is needed in each situation in our own lives. We need to look at our own "Martha–Mary scale" and seek God's discernment. Is this the time to sit back, worship, and reflect on where you are on your journey with Jesus, or is it a time to focus on what God is asking you to do on His behalf? Seek His wisdom. Jesus did say He would give us this gift if only we ask.

How "Free to Be"?

The purpose of the following testimony is to explain where the expression "free to be" was birthed:

The weekend of March 25–28, 1999, began as my wife Anne and I boarded a flight from Jacksonville, Florida, to our destination city to lead a church retreat and healing service. As a side note, our journey took us through Atlanta, as had been the case with many of our other journeys. When we arrived in Atlanta for our connecting flight, we were advised that it was canceled! With a smile on my face, I announced to Anne, "This is going to be a fantastic weekend—if we get there!" We were placed on an Atlanta-to-Cincinnati flight with a change to our ultimate goal. Fortunately, when we called our host from Atlanta, he was about to head for the airport to greet us. We arrived a couple of hours late. God did get us there. The worship for that weekend was outstanding. The Holy Spirit showed up mightily!

As it happens frequently at these weekend teachings, we seemed to connect with a young woman at the service. She had been emotionally wounded as a small girl growing up with sexual abuse within her family. Because of her past, she would not allow men to be part of her present or future. No touching! As she talked and shared with me, she was released of all the painful emotional and physical memories of her past! She even asked if I would hold her with the love of Jesus! The barriers of fear and her fear of rejection melted away from her! How awesome of God!

During the Sunday worship service, there was an invitation for anyone to share how the weekend had spoken to them. This young woman was sitting with us near the back of the sanctuary. I watched her as she leapt out of the pew and began running to the altar as fast as her little legs would allow. With a beautiful smile, she shouted all the way, "I am free! I am free! I am free to be!" Somehow I knew that God, through the love of our Jesus and with the gentle power of the Holy Spirit, was asking me to share this story with as many of you as possible. As you read through this small book, you are called to proclaim *your* freedom as you recognize God's claim upon your life that you are free to be.

I want to share with you one of our addictions. Anne and I seem to be addicted to watching old movies on TV, many from our past. I recall my family of origin's Friday evening dinner rituals with our Sabbath blessings when I was a boy. Our maternal grandparents lived with us. After the meal, Grandpa would ask me, my older sister, and my younger brother if we had been good during the week. We knew what was coming next as he gave each of us a dime to head for the neighborhood movie theater on Saturday afternoon. Seeing these movies again, I became fixated on the language. In these films, whenever an adult is introduced to another, the question is always asked, "How do you *do*?" It seems this is a ritualistic greeting question. In the context of the movies, even kids played by actors such as Mickey Rooney and Judy Garland always greet adults with "How do you *do*?" I learned that as well!

In my early days of going to parties (cocktail or otherwise), I noticed it was usual for the females to meet in one circle of influence and discuss their kids as well as emotions and/or issues! Seldom were they interested in "What do you *be*?"

I will share a recent event in my life that may explain this point. I received a beautiful email from my "spiritual son" from Jacksonville, Florida. Obviously, I am quite close to him, and he did give me permission to quote this short missive. He wrote, "God told me He was very fond of me. I couldn't figure out why He felt that way. Haven't really *done* anything in my life to deserve such an accolade, but I'll surely take it!" The point I made to my "son" is that God is more interested in your *being* than in your *doing*. I know this individual's heart for God, and he does connect with God in his being.

I am reminded of my lifestyle of attending house parties in my twenties (maybe my thirties as well?). It was almost like clockwork: as guests arrived, the guys and gals would split into two different groups and go off to two different locations. Even the topics of conversation were different! The gals would share their thoughts, but mostly their feelings—their "being." However, after discussing weather and/or sports scores, the guys would always ask, "What do you do [for a living]?"—our "doing."

Let us be certain that we are discussing the same subject of freedom. What this word means to one person may not be what it means to another. I am not referring to the secular meaning of this word when I discuss freedom. According to the *American Heritage Dictionary*, the word *freedom* means "the condition of being free." The definition of *free* is as follows: "At liberty; not bound or constrained. Not under obligation or necessity. Costing nothing. Not affected by a given condition or circumstance, etc."

This is *not* the definition I have learned from God's Word. Let us compare:

First, to be totally free, we are "bound." We are bound to the lordship of Jesus, who has indeed set us free to be. Without this bond, there can be no freedom.

Second, we have an obligation to our Lord Jesus when we are free indeed. Freedom does not mean we are free to do whatever we desire or whatever feels good. That seems to be the guideline of too many people today. Freedom requires responsibility to God and our neighbor.

Third, the idea that it costs nothing or is not affected by a given condition or circumstance does not hold water in regard to God's concept of freedom. There *is* a cost! Praise God, the cost was paid on a hill called Calvary, and it was a very expensive price. Likewise, there is a cost that must be paid daily as we are called to pick up our cross and follow Him. There is a cost as we are called to die to self on a daily basis. Yes, the call to freedom does have a price tag, but the benefits are *heavenly*!

What does it mean to be free? The Israelites were led into freedom by Moses as told in the book of Exodus. This event is celebrated every year by the Jewish people in the God-commanded festival called Passover, the Feast of Unleavened Bread (see Leviticus 23:4–8). Although this was an event for the Israelites that supposedly brought them from slavery into freedom, they remained in rebellious spiritual bondage in the desert for forty years. They were *not* free! They are not free now! I recall the last of the well-known Four Questions asked at the Seder meal: "Why do we recline at the table at Passover?" The response is that to recline at the table is a sign of a free person.

Another symbol of a free person can be found in the story of the prodigal son as told in Luke 15:11–32. As the younger son was being received back into the family, the father gave him three gifts: a ring, a robe, and a pair of sandals. The robe was a sign of honor, and the ring was a sign of authority. Sandals were the sign of a *free* person as only slaves went barefoot. The father was telling his son that he no longer was a slave to unforgiveness. (Recall the African American spiritual sung during the Civil War, "All God's Chillun Got Shoes." The black soldiers knew that shoes were a sign of freedom!)

It is ironic that the One who sets us free is indeed "the Lamb of God who takes away the sins of the world." In 1

Corinthians 5:7, Paul refers to Jesus as our Passover Lamb! The unblemished male Lamb that is called to be sacrificed is now the only One that brings us into freedom—the reason for celebrating the Passover.

In the Exodus or Passover story you find that even with God liberating the Israelites from slavery, there was much grumbling and murmuring in the desert. Some of this even began before their crossing of the Red Sea! The people who were called to freedom were unsure who they might become in this new calling. They were uncomfortable with the unknown, whereas they had been comfortable knowing who they were as slaves. To walk into freedom is to make the decision to walk into freedom.

This is so similar to what happens when Jesus calls us to walk into freedom today. Many people are too comfortable in their old lifestyles or settings and therefore say no to the unknown. Instead of rejoicing, they become despondent and even depressed. Yet, Jesus can and will liberate us from this oppression.

There is also a similarity with the history of the United States, when in 1863 Abraham Lincoln signed the Emancipation

Proclamation. This document set all slaves free in this country, and yet many slaves chose to stay in physical bondage because it was the known in their lives. Even the African American slaves had to make a decision to walk in freedom. Some chose not to participate. Even after the close of the Civil War, many black slaves chose to remain in the South with their so-called landlords. In that setting, they knew their identity. To be free was something they could not envision. We also have to make the decision to receive freedom in Jesus or to remain in slavery to sin.

We cannot receive freedom without any tension between *responsibility* and *obedience*. There always needs to be this tension between freedom *and* responsibility. A diagram similar to a seesaw may help to explain this dynamic:

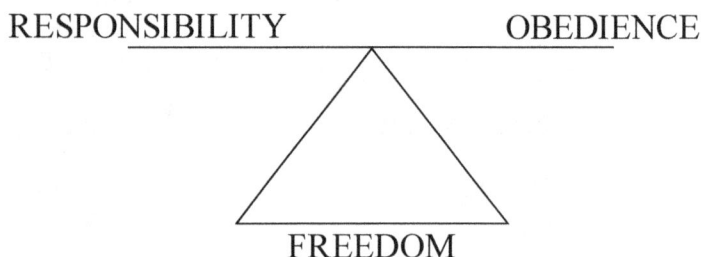

RESPONSIBILITY   OBEDIENCE

FREEDOM

The late Swedish world leader Dag Hammarskjold wrote, "To become free and responsible. For this alone was man created, and he who fails to take the Way which could have been his shall be lost eternally."

A well-known quote of Eleanor Roosevelt is, "Freedom makes a huge requirement of every human being. With freedom comes responsibility."

We need to be aware that obedience and responsibility have to be in balance. So-called "blind obedience" is to be questioned. Perhaps the one who has truly captured the meaning of what it means to be free is the martyred theologian Dietrich Bonhoeffer. Reverend Bonhoeffer was visiting in the United States when World War II broke out. Rather than remain here for the duration, he chose to return to his native Germany to voice his opposition to the evil in his nation. He was arrested, sent to prison, and finally executed shortly before the liberation of his prison camp in 1945. Dietrich Bonhoeffer's book *Letters and Papers from Prison* has become a classic study in what it means to be free—even in the midst of physical imprisonment and with a sentence of death. Bonhoeffer defines the free man as follows: "Who stands fast? Only the man whose final standard is not his reason, his principles, his conscience, his freedom, or his virtue, but who is ready to sacrifice all this when he is called to obedient and responsible action in faith and in exclusive allegiance to God—the responsible man, who tries to make his whole life an answer to the question and call of God."

To further explain the tension between obedience and freedom, as well as responsibility, Bonhoeffer writes, "Responsibility and freedom are corresponding concepts. Responsibility is the freedom of men which is given only in the obligation to God and our neighbor. The action of the responsible man is performed in the obligation which alone gives freedom and which gives entire freedom, the obligation to God and to our neighbor as they confront us in Jesus Christ." He further states, "Obedience without freedom is slavery; freedom without obedience is arbitrary self-will. In responsibility both obedience and freedom are realized. Responsibility implies tension between obedience and freedom." (See previous diagram.)

I believe the person living in freedom with Jesus Christ embraces both life and death; I believe this person actually sees life as a "terminal celebration." To this person, the expression

"To live is to die; to die is to live" has great meaning. This person is the one who freely receives and freely gives. This person will have no fears. Why fear finances? Why fear abandonment? Why fear Satan's whims? Why fear loneliness? Why fear death?

To live without fear is to be free!

To live in responsibility to God and neighbor is to be free!

To live in obedience to God is to be free! (As Dietrich Bonhoeffer wrote, "Only he who obeys truly believes; only he who believes truly obeys.")

The Exodus from Egypt did not make us free; the events of July 4, 1776, in the United States did not make us free; the event at Gettysburg, Pennsylvania, in 1863 did not make us free; the signing of an armistice in November 11, 1918, did not make us free. It is only the event at Calvary that has truly set us free. When we can comprehend not only in our heads, but also primarily in our hearts, what took place on the hill of Calvary on our behalf, then we can learn to embrace our gift of freedom.

In the epistle of James, we find steps to freedom. James 4:7–10 reads as follows: "Submit yourselves, then, to God. Resist the devil and he will flee from you. Come near to God and He will come near to you. Wash your hands, you sinners, and purify your hearts, you double-minded. Grieve, mourn, and wail. Change your laughter into mourning and your joy to gloom. Humble yourselves before the Lord, and He will lift you up."

Let us review the action words in this passage, and then we will have our steps to freedom:

1. Submit

2. Resist

3. Come

4. Wash

5. Purify

6. Grieve (mourn and wail)

7. Humble yourself (exercise humility).

The first directive is to submit. This is a total submission and not just a submitting of a part of oneself. It is a total surrender to God. We have come to believe that to use the word *surrender* is to admit to defeat, whereas in God's kingdom it is a word of victory. What a different concept! It is at this time of total surrender, giving up of self and giving God control of our lives, that we begin to experience true freedom.

Second, we are called to resist and turn away from evil. "Resist the devil," as James puts it. This is a resistance of things yet to come our way from the pit of hell. I also believe it could be a call to repentance of things in our past. We need to be reminded that German theologian Dietrich Bonhoeffer called forgiveness without repentance a "cheap grace."

The next step to freedom is crucial: come near to God. How often we hear the quotation to "resist the devil and he will flee from you," but then do not hear the rest of the sentence. After resisting, we are called, perhaps commanded, to come near to God and He will come near to us. How comforting to know that as we draw near to Him, He will draw near to us! We cannot continue our journey into freedom without drawing closer and closer to the One who has beckoned us into freedom.

The next part of our entrance into freedom with Jesus Christ is to wash and purify. This ties into the ancient custom of the Hebrew people, which is still practiced today by the Orthodox Jews, to cleanse themselves in the ceremonial ritual bath. This was done even before Holy Scriptures could be read. For our freedom journey, James tells us we need more than an "outer cleansing"; we need an "inner cleansing" as well. This is a heart purification that takes place.

As James tells us to "grieve, mourn, and wail," I do not believe he is advising us to be gloom-and-doom Christians as we grow in and rely on Christ. Actually, the opposite occurs as the free Christian will find sources of joy it has never experienced before. There is nothing artificial about this true joy. We cannot start the journey, however, without acknowledging the sinful nature of all of us. For any of us who once loved what the world has to offer, we go through this period of grieving, mourning, and wailing. It is on the other side of this that we understand the words of Jesus as found in Matthew 5:4: "Blessed are those who mourn, for they will be comforted."

Let us review the steps to freedom as found in this letter: *Submit* into a loving relationship with our Lord Jesus. We are to *resist* the attempts of the "accuser of the brethren" to lie to us and/or falsely accuse us of things in our past. We are called to participate with God in a *cleansing* of our hearts, recognizing any unconfessed sin in our lives and taking it before God. Remember that Jesus is our Mediator and our Advocate to the Father. We are to continue to *draw near* to God and allow Him to draw near to us, and as this takes place, we are to seek *humility* in our lives.

So, you have made the decision to journey into freedom with Jesus. Will it be smooth sailing from now on? Do you remember step two from above, to resist the devil and he will flee from you? If it is indeed smooth sailing along the road, why would we need to resist the devil? Does Satan accompany us along this pathway? Are there stumbling blocks or even booby traps along this path? Is this to be like the road traveled in Paul Bunyan's classic book *Pilgrim's Progress*?

What are some of the snares we might expect? In the next chapter, we will take a realistic look at what may be the "things to come." What may we expect as barriers to freedom?

Ponder Page

1. Reflect on your childhood for your "once upon a time" event. Are the memories good or painful? (Remember, God will set you free of the hurtful memories.)

2. Do you sense or feel yoked to Jesus? If not, lift up this request to God now.

3. Reread "Five Short Chapters." At which phase do you find yourself? What will it take on your part to reach the point where you are "walk[ing] down a different street"?

4. Do you feel that your knowing, being, and doing is balanced in a godly way in your life?

Chapter 2

Stumbling Blocks

> It is for freedom that Christ has set us free. Stand firm, then, and do not let yourselves be burdened again by a yoke of slavery. ... You, my brothers, were called to be free. Do not use your freedom to indulge in sinful nature; rather serve one another in love.
> —Galatians 5:1, 5:13

God desires us to be free.

God needs us to be free.

God calls us to be free.

No doubt, there will be roadblocks on your path to God's freedom. Many are the snares that the evil one has placed in our paths. Let's spend some time looking at these barriers, to keep you on the road to His calling you to be free to be. My first challenge in putting these words together is to emphasize the reason for *Free to Be*: God's Word calls us to freedom—and freedom with Him. His calling to you is that you live free and be the one He created you to be!

As I begin this section on stumbling blocks, I open with a prayer:

I pray through God's love and the power of His Holy Spirit that the reader hears the intent of this chapter and the whole of *Free to Be*. It is not critical of anyone's belief or ministry, including the ministries of healing, inner healing, deliverance, and reconciliation, for which You, God, have so graciously anointed my wife Anne and me. Throughout Your written Word, you emphasize the healing love and touch that You have for all. I am thankful for this. I believe you are guiding me only so that I may see Your intent to heal all of us and "set the captives free." Your healing love will indeed be a huge step for Your children to take in order to be free to be in the mighty healing name of Jesus. Amen.

Robert Kennedy wrote the following pertaining to our freedom: "I can understand the Chinese Wall: It was built as a defense against marauders. But a wall such as that in Berlin, built to prevent people from seeking freedom, is almost beyond comprehension."

God's gift of healing is a huge stepping-stone on our road to becoming free to be.

Living free with Jesus is what we seek. I rejoice in the works of the Holy Spirit. I am only sharing with you through my eyes, ears, and spirit that this is a large and major step to begin walking into freedom with Jesus, our Messiah.

During our journey of God's ministry to set captives free through healings, Anne and I have been mentored over these forty-plus years by spiritual giants such as Francis and Judith MacNutt, Dennis and Rita Bennett, John and Paula Sanford, and Ruth Carter Stapleton. We also have attended healing seminars taught by David Seamands and Tom White, among others. Now I present the following is a checklist of stumbling blocks for you to consider on your own journey:

Sin

Although I personally thoroughly enjoyed the movie *Born Free* and have seen it numerous times, I must say that we really are not born free. I have frequently heard the statement that we are born with an addiction called sin.

If only we believed and programmed our lives to live through the Holy Scriptures! I have no intention of hitting anyone over the head with a Bible. "If only we believed!" It is all written and emphasized in God's Word. There are sermons being said weekly (weakly?) of God's redeeming atonement of our sinful nature. Again, I repeat: "If only we believed."

This short statement takes me back to the classic George Burns movie *Oh, God!* There is a great line in the movie when the grocery clerk, played by John Denver, is explaining to his wife his God encounter. When she questions him, he asks, "Don't you believe in God?" Her quick response is, "Yes, I believe in God! I just don't think He exists."

Since a few may doubt that God, through the sacrifice of His Son Jesus, our Messiah, has set us free of sin—past, present, and future—there is still struggle with sin. Perhaps it is believed that freedom from sin is "for the other guy, whereas I don't deserve this freedom and grace that comes with responsibility." When Anne and I were active in the ministry of healing and reconciliation, we usually made the statement at the end of the day, "If only our clients believed their sins are forgiven and freedom awaits them, we would be out of a job!" Dr. Karl Menninger, a famous psychiatrist from Topeka, Kansas, who founded the Menninger Clinic in the 1920s, published a classic book in 1973, probably still in print, titled *Whatever Became of Sin?* He recognized that society no longer recognizes sin as sin. One of his many quoted expressions states that if he could convince his patients at the clinic that they were forgiven of their sins, more than 75 percent of them could walk out that day. "If only we believed."

Healing of Hurtful Memories

In my anguish I cried to the Lord, and He answered by setting me free.
—Psalm 118:5

Most important is to assume your own attitude of prayer. Ask God through the power of the Holy Spirit to reveal anything in your past that could give rise to hurtful memories. This goes back to the beginning of your memories, even those from when you were an infant. Do not be concerned if nothing comes to mind immediately. God knows your heart and your emotions. There are times when the Holy Spirit knows there may be memories that are too painful to be revealed at this time. Just sit back, relax, and know that God is in charge. These memories may be stored deep within you. Sometimes it's helpful to see this process with God as taking one layer at a time, like peeling an onion one layer at a time.

What wounding words do you recall? "I'm stupid"; "I'll never amount to anything"; "God couldn't possibly love me";

"I'm damaged beyond repair"; etc. You may want to make a list of these and then give God the entire list for His healing and freedom. God reminds us in Paul's teaching in Ephesians 3:16–19: "I pray that from his glorious, unlimited recourses he will empower you with inner strength through his Spirit. Then Christ will make his home in your hearts as you trust in him. Your roots will grow down into God's love and keep you strong. And may you have the power to understand, as all God's people should, how wide, how long, how high, and how deep his love is."

Ask God to show you any painful visions from your past. I'll share one of mine that had haunted me since I was in first grade class in Saint Louis. To explain how this event has controlled me, I'll have you know that all my adult life I had a fear of speaking up in a group meeting of any kind. It was too painful to even think about doing this. I was okay with a one-on-one conversation, but in a group, it was nothing doing. During a time of prayer, I saw myself as a six-year-old in the first grade. I can still see my teacher and even remember her name. If a student gave a wrong answer to a question from the teacher, he or she was sent to the cloakroom in the back of the class. I must have given numerous wrong answers as I saw myself spending a lot of time in that cloakroom!

During this time of seeing myself sitting alone at a desk in the cloakroom, I saw Jesus enter the cloakroom and walk toward me, but He did not stop (rejected again?). He walked to the back wall, where I saw my teacher. Jesus approached her, looked at her face-to-face, gave her a hug, and turned toward me. Although he did not stop, Jesus held out his hand. I grabbed it, and we walked out of the cloakroom together. Since that Spirit-filled event in my imagination, God has set me free to be relieved of any fear of speaking in groups of any size. I even remember speaking to almost a thousand church attendees in England years ago—with no problems. This healing event in my life opened me to the hundreds of teachings I have done in churches. A big "Praise the Lord" for me and others.

A popular worship song called "I Will Change Your Name," by the group Eden's Bridge, recorded in 1998, has helped many people in our ministry. It is a time for God to change your name, putting away your old name from the past and bringing to the foreground what He will call you today:

I will change, will change your name.

I will change, will change your name.
You shall no longer be called
Wounded, outcast, lonely or afraid.
I will change your name.
Your new name shall be
Confidence, joyfulness, overcoming one.

As an example of the power of this song, I share with you the following testimony: A woman came to see us for ministry for her low self-esteem. She had heard many accusations growing up that had caused her to develop a terrible self-image, see herself as very homely, and convince her that she would never amount to anything as an adult. She had programmed herself for failure. We asked her to come back to see us, saying that we wanted to play this song for her to see if God would give her a new name, a new self-image. She agreed, and that's just what we did when she returned a week later.

We opened in prayer, asking God to speak to her with the name He would call her instead of confronting her with the lies she had heard about herself. We also told her that this was something between her and her God—not a name we would give her! Upon hearing and focusing upon this song speaking only to her, she became radiant and smiled. She even started laughing! Our curiosity got the best of us, and we asked, "What is happening?" Her beautiful response was that God truly had given her a new name that He would call her from that moment on. Her new name was Hope. And, yes, she claimed her new name and began living in hope instead of gloom! Allow the Holy Spirit to change your name if need be.

I would like to address the aspect of anger in terms of hurtful memories. Presently, we are living in a nation full of anger, which leads to bitterness and finally to hate and rage. Something usually triggers anger within us. One of the many things Anne and I have learned from our experience in helping people deal with their anger is to discuss what triggers this emotion. We usually find it is triggered by one of three causes: hurt, fear, or unmet needs. Sometimes it's all three. When the person asks the Holy Spirit to reveal what triggered the cause, again with the guidance of the Spirit of God, the anger dissipates.

If you desire more information pertaining to the healing of memories or any other topic related to these stumbling blocks, please take a look at the bibliography in the back matter. Some of the authors cited there may have ministries that can offer assistance to you. If your church has a ministry of caring, you may want to discuss this with them. There are numerous anointed ministries you can look into for help, such as Christian Healing Ministries in Jacksonville, Florida. Some may also have the ability to meet with you over Zoom.

Physical Healings

Although our God does many physical healings, He tells us the following in James 5:14–15: "Are any of you sick? You should call for the elders of the church to come and pray over you, anointing you with oil in the name of the Lord. Such a prayer offered in faith will heal the sick, and the Lord will make you well." I have purposely decided not to spend much time on this topic of physical healing. If you are ill, seek anointed people in your local church to pray for you. Like you the reader, I too have seen many people with physical impediments who have become victorious overcomers and powerful witnesses for our Lord. He can use our so-called "handicaps" to bring glory to Himself. (A great example of this is something my dad went through, which I will share with you later in *Free to Be*.)

Unforgiveness

Unforgiveness (grudges?) in your life will always be a stumbling block on your road to freedom. When someone hurts us with words and/or deeds, too often we want revenge. We find it almost too difficult to release the perpetrator who wounded us. Yet, to release the person is exactly what God requires of us.

After the disciples of Jesus ask him how to pray, he teaches them what we refer to as "the Lord's Prayer," as found in Matthew 6:9–13. Then in verse 14, which follows, we find Jesus's instructions for how to pray. He concludes with one of his many powerful postscripts: "If you forgive those who sin against you, your heavenly Father will forgive you. But if you refuse to forgive others, your Father will not forgive your sins." It is quite clear that if you will not forgive those who have wounded you, you are the one in bondage and will not be set free. No "free to be" until you repent of your grudges and ask your heavenly Father for forgiveness.

My beloved wife Anne is such a strong example of the power of unforgiveness in our lives and of what possibilities open to us when we take our unforgiveness to God. Anne and

I first met at an Episcopal renewal conference in Louisville, Kentucky, many years ago. At the time, she was crippled with arthritis so badly that her friends or daughters needed to help her get dressed and undressed. It was even difficult for her to hold a toothbrush or cut food at mealtimes.

At this conference, an Episcopal priest asked her about any unforgiveness in her life. After going through a checklist of possibilities, it was revealed that she still felt bitterness, hurt, pain, and anger toward her mother. Upon confession of this, there was a time for repentance and release of all unforgiveness to God. The following morning, Anne's colleagues from Michigan called to her attention that she was sitting on the floor, something she previously had not been able to do. After a time of celebration and going through some gyrations of her arms and legs, it was obvious that Anne had been set free of her painful and crippling arthritis by her giving of her unforgiveness to God. Another PTL.

False Teachings (Doctrines)

Throughout my lifetime, I have encountered numerous false teachings from false prophets. I do believe most of the time that these people are unaware that their teachings are not scriptural. There are many warnings throughout scripture to be prepared for false teachings and prophets. Believing in these falsehoods will keep us off the path of being set free. Focus upon a few of God's teachings and ask the Holy Spirit, the giver of truth and wisdom, to be your guide.

- "Beware, false prophets who come disguised as false messiahs and false prophets will rise up and perform great signs and wonders so as to deceive, if possible, even God's chosen ones. See, I have warned you about this ahead of time" (Mark 13:22–23).

- "But I will continue doing what I have always done. This will undercut those who are looking for an opportunity to boast that their work is just like ours. These people are false apostles. They are deceitful workers who disguise themselves as apostles of Christ" (2 Corinthians 11:12–13).

- "But there were also false prophets in Israel, just as there will be false teachers among you. They will cleverly teach destructive heresies and even deny the Master who bought them. In this way, they will bring sudden destruction on themselves. Many will follow their evil teaching and shameful immortality. And because of these teachers, the way of truth will be slandered. In their greed they will make up clever lies to get hold of your money. But God condemned them long ago, and their destruction will not be delayed" (2 Peter 2:1–3).

Demonic Activity

And you will know the truth, and the truth will set you truly free. ... So, if the Son sets you free, you are truly free.
—John 8:32, 8:36

Make a list of any demonic activity you may have engaged in. Although there are checklists available through various ministries, such as Christian Healing Ministries in Jacksonville, Florida, you can also ask the Holy Spirit to reveal any practices from your past that may have been displeasing to your Lord. I did this years ago, and the first thing that popped into my mind was a memory of my older sister and me innocently playing with a Ouija board! Interesting that Amazon still sells this as a "Spirit Board" or a "Spirit Hunt." No wonder my God was displeased with me. I needed to ask for His forgiveness pronto! God then revealed something to me. After my marriage to Anne, we both resided in Michigan for a time so as to learn where God may want us to live: perhaps in Anne's beautiful home in Michigan, or possibly in my apartment in Middletown, Kentucky, with the possibility of owning a home in nearby Oldham County. We even consulted a person involved with reading tea leaves to forecast or predict our future. Maybe that was strike two for me? I do not think God is keeping score on me. This was another event in my life when I was seeking wisdom, knowledge, and direction from a spirit other than the Holy Spirit. And this was another time to go through my list of Five R's, as follows:

- Recognize

  Obviously, I needed to recognize where I went off track and offended God. Had I attended spiritual séances? worshipped other gods? sought help from the netherworld? visited someone who used a crystal ball to guide me? As mentioned when talking about my own journey, you should ask the Holy Spirit to bring forward any activities you engaged in that were displeasing to God and opposed to His Word.

- Renounce

  Openly in prayer, renounce all demonic activities, known and unknown at this time, that would be displeasing to God. This is a time of cleansing, time to take a "spiritual shower." (At times, I can picture standing in a shower and allowing the soothing living waters of God's Holy Spirit to flow over me, with all that needs cleansing flowing down the drain.)

- Rebuke

  Rebuke all activities in the mighty and healing name of Jesus. Express this loudly, if possible, and with someone you trust who will walk through this with you. A reminder from 1 John 38b: "But the Son of God came to destroy the works of the devil." I also suggest you read and absorb into your spirit Paul's words found in Galatians 5:7–10. "You were running the race so well. Who has held you back from following the truth?

It certainly isn't God, for He is the one who called you to freedom. This false teaching is like a little yeast that spreads through the whole batch of dough! I am trusting the Lord to keep you from believing false teachings. God will judge that person, whoever he is, who has been confusing you."

Also read Romans 16:20 to remind Satan of his destiny: "The God of Peace will soon crush Satan under your feet." We also have the reminder that all is possible when we walk with God. See Mark 9:23, where Jesus reminds us, "Anything is possible if a person believes."

- Repent

  The entire Bible, from the Old(er) Testament through the New(er) Testament, is a history of God's calling us to repentance. It is the doorway into the experience of His love and grace. Repentance was the message of John the Baptist, and it was mentioned in the words of Jesus, Paul, and the apostles who carried that message throughout the region: "Repent, for the kingdom of God is at hand!"

- Rejoice

    It is a time to celebrate these new steps you have taken. This is like taking that spiritual shower again. It is always a time for celebration and rejoicing when you walk away from Satan's snares by using these Five R's. I always get a boost when I latch on to one of my favorite scriptures from Paul. Philippians 4:4 reminds me, "Always be full of joy in the Lord. I say it again— rejoice!" Rejoice! Don't ever stop. Satan can't handle it!

A Testimony of Healing and Deliverance

Saginaw, Michigan, October 1985

(*Note:* For purposes of privacy, the person's name has been changed.)

This event took place at an International Order of Saint Luke the Physician conference in Saginaw, Michigan. On the last morning of the conference, my wife Anne and I were leading. The regional chaplain for the meeting was our friend Reverend Mainert Peterson of Louisville, Kentucky.

Jane walked with both her legs in braces and seemed somewhat retarded in her speech. Her mother asked if we would pray for her legs to be healed before the conference ended. It was during one of our break times that we met in the library. God revealed to us that we were dealing with something demonic.

As we called upon the name of Jesus Christ and commanded Satan to release his hold upon Jane, we noticed that she was dealing with pain in her legs. She wanted to stop because of the pain, so I just held her for a few moments. It was my hope and prayer that she would feel the unconditional love of Jesus flowing into her. I prayed for Jane as I was holding her in my arms. She gave the okay to continue the prayers of deliverance, at which time she witnessed that the pain was leaving her legs and flowing up into her torso. It seemed to be lodged in her body. I continued to give her words of encouragement, as well as commands that she could speak to Satan. (I added that it would be beneficial if she were to participate with us and express her need to have this demon leave her.) I noticed she could not handle longer sentences. I therefore broke these up into short phrases for her. She revealed to us that she had recalled her trip to Ireland when her health began to deteriorate and went from bad to much worse. We sensed a family curse placed upon her. Jane did indeed come up with several names of family members who may have thusly been cursed. We prayed against these family curses in Jesus's name, and with Jane's help, the pain began to move upward once again. She kept gritting her teeth, squeezing my hand, and saying, "Come on, Jesus. Come on, Jesus. Come on, Jesus." She began coughing in a seemingly uncontrollable way. This lasted for several minutes, then silence, then keen discernment that "something left." We prayed for the Holy Spirit to fill any void in her precious body with His love, peace, and joy.

God's timing is *always* perfect! Just as we ended our time with Jane, we were informed that the last session of teaching needed to begin in the conference room. We asked our new friend to stay in the library and rest since she had just gone through "spiritual surgery" and her body needed to be restored and refreshed.

After our last session, we all adjourned to the dining room for our last meal together as a group. During the lunch, all eyes fell upon Jane as she entered the room *carrying her leg braces*! She announced to the entire group that she was taking her leg braces home with her to use as planters for ivy to grow up. As she was speaking to the group, it was obvious that she was speaking in sentences rather than the short type of phrases she needed to use previously. There seemed to be no sign of retardation in her speech. We praise God for what He did for Jane that day!

Whenever I hear the part of the Lord's Prayer that says "deliver us from evil" (or "from the evil one"), I think of Jane. God truly wants us to be set free! He sent His Son to set the captives free! We can claim we are free to be.

Fear(s)

> Such love has no fear, because perfect love expels
> all fear.
> —1 John 4–18

I put an *s* in parentheses after the word *fear* to be sure it is in the plural. I believe many people are riddled with fears. Since I grew up in the years of Franklin Delano Roosevelt's presidency, I still remember his speech about fear where he said, "So, first of all, let me assert my firm belief that the only thing we have to fear is fear itself—nameless, unreasoning, unjustified terror that paralyzes needed efforts to convert retreat into advance." Approximately eighty-five years later, many of us still struggle with fear. The author David Icke wrote the following: "The greatest prison people live in is the fear of what people think." How true!

Fear can be crippling when it overpowers us and affects our emotions. It can even cripple our decision-making process. On the flip side, it can save our lives. Fear can stop us from stepping out in front of a fast-moving truck. It can be that inner voice telling us not to go in a particular direction. Rely on the power of God's Holy Spirit to guide you and direct you, as He has promised He will be there.

In my own journey into freedom, it took me time to turn all my fears over to God and see them dissolve. It was a gradual process, with progress made over a period of time. I believe what sped up the progression for me was spending equal time in God's Word and His promises for me. It seemed that for each fear I tackled, He revealed to me a biblical Word. The more I read the Word of God, the faster my fears succumbed to His Word! I still focus on 1 John 4:18: "Such love has no fear, because perfect love expels all fear." I find God's personal promises to me by reading the words of the prophet Isaiah: "Don't be afraid, for I am with you. Don't be discouraged, for

I am your God. I will strengthen you and help you. I will hold you up with my victorious right hand" (Isaiah 41:10). Isaiah even informs me that God paid a ransom for me!

When I went through roughly seven months of unemployment many years ago, I was overwhelmed with fear for myself and my entire family. Fortunately, Joshua was/is one of my biblical heroes. I still enjoy reading his farewell address. Read chapters 23 and 24 of the book of Joshua—a powerful message! When God is giving Joshua His directions to go forth after the death of Moses, He gives instructions too, as found in Joshua 1:7–9: "Be strong and courageous. Study this book of instruction [the Word of God] continually. Meditate upon it day and night so you will be sure to obey everything written in it. Only then will you prosper and succeed in all you do. This is my command— be strong and courageous! Do not be afraid or discouraged. For the Lord your God is with you wherever you go."

We can overcome the fear of fear. As you learned when I was speaking of my own journey, there will be times when fear can feel overwhelming and even seem like a prison. I have learned that there is even a game on the internet called *Castle of Fear*. There also have been several books written with this title.

If you find yourself in this prison of fear, you will learn the fact that most of the time, the door to the prison cell is not even locked. All that is required for you to leave is simply to visualize yourself arising from your cell, walking to the door, and walking out for good! For others, it is not quite so easy.

You find yourself bruised and even bleeding from your wrists, where the shackles have been for such a long time. You have even tried opening the cell door, but it is too heavy for you to open. Your thoughts turn to "if only": *If only someone would help me! I cannot do this on my own weakened strength. I ache too much from this painful torment.*

As you slowly turn your head back to the prison door, you begin to see the image of someone standing outside the cell of fear. As you continue to focus on the person and less upon yourself, you finally see it is Jesus with his hand extended toward you. He is waving for you to get up, go to the door, and walk out into His outstretched arms. With His smile of compassion and encouragement, you slowly walk out of the bondage of fear!

I am free—free at last of this bondage to fear. To be certain I do not return to this musty prison cell, I begin to ask Jesus for

His forgiveness for my not believing in His Father's words: "My perfect love casts out *all* fears" (1 John 4:18; emphasis added). Yes, I am now free to be!

Attitude

If your attitude is dragging a bit, you will need an attitude boost. The first suggestion is to focus on Paul's proclamation found in Philippians 4:19: "And this same God who takes care of me will supply all your needs from his glorious riches, which have been given to us in Christ Jesus." What a great word of encouragement to renew a slipping attitude. Also, read what Charles Swindoll says about our attitude:

> The longer I live, the more I realize the impact of attitude on my life. Attitude, to me, is more important than facts. It is more important than the past, than education, than money, than circumstances, than failures, than successes, than whatever people think or say or do. It is more important than appearance, giftedness, or skill. It will make or break a company, a school, a home. The remarkable thing is that we have a choice every day regarding the attitude we will embrace for the day. We cannot change our past. We cannot change the fact that people will act in a certain way. We cannot change the inevitable. The only thing we can do is play on the one thing

we have, and that is our attitude …. I am convinced that life is 10 percent what happens to me and 90 percent how I react to it.

God's promise is that He can and will renew your attitude toward walking out in freedom with Him. Step out in faith as Joshua did in his farewell: "As for me and my family, we *will* serve the Lord!" (Joshua 24:15; emphasis added). When your attitude is attempting to convince you that you are unqualified, or the next time you feel like God can't use you, remember the following people:

- Noah—a drunk
- Abraham—too old
- Isaac—a daydreamer
- Jacob—a liar
- Leah—homely
- Joseph—abused
- Moses—fearful of talking
- Gideon—afraid
- Sampson—a longhaired womanizer
- Rahab—a prostitute

- Jeremiah and Timothy—too young

- David—an adulterer and murderer

- Elijah—suicidal and depressed

- Isaiah—who preached naked

- Jonah—who ran from God

- Job—who went bankrupt

- John the Baptist—who ate insects

- Peter—who denied Christ

- The disciples—who fell asleep while praying

- Martha—a worrier

- Mary Magdalene—demon possessed

- The Samaritan woman—divorced more than once and now living with another man

- Zacchaeus—too small

- Paul—too religious

- Timothy—who had an ulcer

- Lazarus—who was dead!

No more excuses! God used all these people mightily. He can use you too!

Go for it with your renewed attitude and with zest (and go

far with it). If you are still breathing as you read this, then God is not finished with you yet.

Misplaced Priorities

With this opportunity, it is now time to check what your priorities are for walking your Christian walk. Sometimes priorities get out of whack as did mine. God seems to have a plan for us about this. He needed to get my attention and get me back on track. God's plan is always to be first in our lives. Here is his list—in proper order:

- God first.
- Spouse second (assuming you are married).
- Children third (if He blesses you with children).
- Rest of family, including in-laws (and "outlaws"; I only mention this because there are times when in-laws attempt to be in control), fourth.
- In fifth place, we find employment. Again, usually among men, we find that a job is top priority. This

area is where God spoke to me about my misplaced priorities!

- And finally, in sixth place, is ministry. For many of us, this is our means of employment.

Losing Your First Love for Jesus

In the second chapter of the book of Revelation, Jesus tells the church at Ephesus that whereas they have developed some good traits, they also are deserving of a strong reprimand. Verses 4–5 strongly say, "But I have this complaint against you. You don't love Me or each other as you did at first. Look how far you have fallen!" Does this stir something in your heart or mind? Have you fallen short of the love you had for Jesus when He first entered your life?

The following story involving my conviction of my love affair with Jesus will expose my thoughts to you:

Prophetic Word to Don at Mayport Chapel

Early 1990s

One of my and Anne's "spiritual sons" was a chaplain at the Mayport naval base in Jacksonville, Florida. He was giving the

Mother's Day sermon at the chapel and invited us to listen to his message. It was indeed a powerful sermon about the blessings of mothers.

Upon my leaving the naval base, God spoke to me quite clearly. My wife Anne recalls my pulling our car off to the side of the road as God spoke to me. His message to me was short and to the point: "I love you!" My natural response was, "I love you, too!" God's clear voice responded with, "You cannot *fathom* my love for you. You can only express love in your earthly expressions of love. I am speaking from my heavenly expression of love."

And now, about forty years later, in a pamphlet written by Sister Joela Kruger of the Evangelical Sisterhood of Mary, in Phoenix, Arizona, I read the following confirmation of what God said to me at Mayport years ago:

"He [God] comforts like a mother, and as a father has compassion on his children, so God has compassion on us. And one day he will wipe away all our tears [Isaiah 55:9, 66:13; Jeremiah 29:11; Psalm 103:13; Revelation 7:17]. Who can even begin to fathom such love? Indeed, it cannot be fathomed, only worshipped."

The following are a couple of quotations from a book written by Basilea Schlink that hopefully will speak to you:

"Love, bridal love! Who can comprehend its secret? It is too deep, too high, too wide for us to ever fully fathom." (My thought: There is that word *fathom* again!)

"Empty your heart of everything filling it, and you will find the most valuable gift, the most wonderful gift in all the world: a love relationship between you and Me—the deepest, closest, holiest, and strongest possible. Surrender all else, and you will find it!"

If some of this stirs your heart, I suggest you read the classic book written more than a century ago by Basilea Schlink, *My All for Him: Fall in Love with Jesus All Over Again*.

God's Words of Encouragement to You

God says, "I will direct your steps" (Proverbs 3:5–6).

You say, "I'm too tired."
God says, "I will give you rest" (Matthew 11:28–30).

You say, "It's impossible."
God says, "All things are possible" (Luke 18:27).

You say, "Nobody really loves me."
God says, "I love you" (John 3:16; 13:34).

You say, "I'm not accepted."
God says, "You did not choose Me, but I chose you"
(John 15:16).

You say, "I feel condemned."
God says, "There is no condemnation for those who
follow Jesus" (Romans 8:1).

You say, "It's not worth it."
God says, "It will be worth it" (Romans 8:28).

You say, "I don't have enough faith."
God says, "I've given everyone a measure of faith"
(Romans 12:3).

You say, "I'm not smart enough."
God says, "I give you wisdom" (1 Corinthians 1:30).

You say, "I'm not able."
God says, "I am able" (2 Corinthians 9:8).

You say, "I can't go on."
God says, "My grace is sufficient" (2 Corinthians 12:9;
Psalm 91:15).

You say, "I can't do it."
God says, "You can do all things" (Philippians 4:13).

You say, "I can't forgive myself."
God says, "I forgive you" (1 John 1:9; Romans 8:1).

You say, "I can't manage."
God says, "I will supply all your needs" (Philippians 4:19).

You say, "I'm afraid."
God says, "I have not given you a spirit of fear" (2 Timothy 1:7).

You say, "I feel all alone."
God says, "I will never leave you nor forsake you" (Hebrews 13:5).

You say, "I'm worried and frustrated."
God says, "Cast all your cares on Me" (1 Peter 5:7).

You say, "My [our] future looks questionable/bleak."
God says, "Seek first the kingdom of God and all these things will be added onto you" (Matthew 6:33).

You say, "Satan may influence my future."
God says, "The thief comes to steal and destroy. I have come to give you life abundantly (overflowing)" (John 10:10).

You say, "God doesn't understand my suffering."
God says, "And the God of all grace, who called you to His eternal glory in Christ, after you have suffered a little while, will Himself restore you and make you strong, firm, and steadfast. To Him, be the power and the glory for ever and ever. Amen" (1 Peter 5:10–11).

Allow God's Word to encourage you. The more you practice seeking God's word, the fewer negative thoughts will filter into your thought life. Graham Cooke, the well-known Christian speaker, made the following powerful statement: "Changing your mindset is the best way to handle a negative circumstance. Don't argue with negativity. Ignore it! Then step forcefully into the mind of Christ to discover his good pleasure." What a powerful method of avoiding Satan's negativity!

As a preteen and a teenager in the 1940s, I often heard a certain popular song. Maybe this was a hit meant to keep our mindsets positive during the early years of World War II when things were not going so well for us. The song's message was to accentuate our positives, eliminate our negative thoughts, and refrain from messing with Mister In-Between—whomever that may be in your life. Do the following three things:

- Accentuate the positives and hang on to them.
- Eliminate the negatives you may be believing.
- Focus on the affirmatives in your life and on the scriptures.

I will walk about in freedom, for I have sought your precepts.
—Psalm 119:45

What Is Self-Image?

Finally, and equally important as all the preceding directives, is healing of our self-image.

What is self-image? When in doubt, we can always turn to our dictionary! *The American Dictionary* defines *self-image* as "one's conception of oneself." Quite simply, this means that whatever I think of myself is my self-image. Your self-image is your own mental picture of yourself.

With this in mind, it becomes quite obvious that our self-image can be much different from the image that others have of us, and also quite different from the image our God has of us. Our life responses are not so much determined by who we are as they are based more on *who we think we are.* Too many people today are living in a private sort of despair or perhaps harbor a feeling of hopelessness because of their poor self-image. This is in direct opposition to the definition of a healthy self-image: "A healthy self-image is seeing yourself as God sees you."

If we do not like the kind of person we are, then we will assume no one else likes us either. Yet our self-image will influence every part of our lives. Keep in mind that a good self-image will give us a feeling of significance and of being worthwhile. The person with a healthy self-image will see his or her role in the world as a challenge and an opportunity. With the grace of God, such people know they can make an impact on their environment and their relationships with others. They see their lives as having a destiny that Jesus Christ will manifest through them. This group of people are living examples of and witnesses to Philippians 4:13: "I can do everything through Him who gives me strength."

On the flip side of this is a poor self-image, which will give a person low self-esteem and a low sense of self-worth and also causing him or her to be fearful, rejected, mistrustful of others, and enslaved to what others may think of him or her. A poor self-image will also lead to other self-defeating behaviors and, most important, will make a person become a prime candidate for Satan's attacks consisting of lies, deceit, and accusations. People with a poor self-image will stumble into Satan's well-prepared pit. They will feel hopelessly trapped in this pit of despair until they allow the penetrating light of *God's* image of them to filter through the dust that Satan has created.

Persons with an unhealthy self-image have a fearful, pessimistic view of the world and are doubtful of their ability to cope with life's challenges. They also see the world as closing in on them, pushing them, and crushing them. They also tend to have an image of themselves as victims.

Following are some questions to ponder about your self-image:

1. Can I easily accept compliments or praise about myself, or do I respond negatively by saying, "That's not me you're talking about"?
2. Do I like the mental picture I have of myself?
3. Do I wish I were a different person than I am?
4. Can I honestly say, "I am worthy"?

List any strong points you see in yourself, and then make a list of your weaknesses. Which list took longer to make? What does this tell you about your self-image?

Let us attempt to gain some clarity on some concepts and definition as we are using some words and expressions interchangeably that have similar meanings. The compound words *self-esteem*, *self-image*, and *self-concept* are all frequently read in the context of counseling literature. The meanings of these words do overlap and interrelate to a large degree.

Dr. Gary Collins, in his classic book *Christian Counseling*, explains this beautifully and simply. He mentions that self-image and self-concept both refer to the mental pictures we have of ourselves. This is how we see ourselves based on many concepts to be discussed later. These are the thoughts and feelings we have about ourselves.

Self-esteem is slightly different in meaning. This is more of an evaluation that an individual makes of his or her own self-worth, competence, and/or significance. Whereas self-image and self-concept involve a self-description and a sense of how we see ourselves, self-esteem involves a self-evaluation to determine how we see our value or worth.

As previously stated, these terms will and do overlap, and I personally do not believe we need to be caught up in definitions. In God's eyes, we all need positive self-esteem, a positive self-concept, and a positive self-image. This is God's intent for us, and many modern approaches to Christian counseling will focus on helping the counselee improve his or her beliefs in all these categories.

Where Does Self-Image Originate?

Although the question asked by the subhead addresses where we receive our self-image, another, similar question to be addressed is "When do we form our self-image?" One's self-image may be formed in one's mother's womb. I will not spend much time on this subject, as it is another teaching entirely. Prenatal prayer therapy is a valid ministry in and of itself as one's self-image may develop in infancy while being carried and cared for within the womb. A fetus may pick up the emotions of its mother. If the parents really do not want the baby, the infant might pick up on the emotion of rejection. The baby might also become confused and unsure of itself if the parents verbally express that they wanted a child of the opposite sex. (I know of some people who were confused about their own sexuality because of this happening in their lives.)

If certain times in the parents' lives are times of fear or insecurity, perhaps because of loss of a job, poor finances, or uncertainty for the future, the infant will feel these same emotions of insecurity, perhaps manifesting in a sense of not being desired or wanted, or as anticipation of the worst happening. One of the most devastating things that can happen to a child is to realize he or she was not wanted!

The author of the book *His Image, My Image*, Josh McDowell, states, "For all of us the foundation begins to be laid the moment the doctor places us in our mother's arms. At that point we start relating to our parents and other members of our family. By the age of five or six our self-concept, the person we think we are in relationship to others, is so firmly established that we will resist efforts to change it."

Another possible source of one's self-image is the traumatic experience of being a child who is separated from his or her primary caregivers—the parents. This might occur because of the death of one parent or both parents, a divorce in the immediate family, or one of a number of other reasons that may cause a child to acquire a *fear of abandonment*. When a child struggles with this fear and is not affirmed, his or her self-image may suffer greatly.

From early childhood, the child assimilates information

from both authority figures and peers. There are three areas in which the child evaluates himself or herself, as follows:

1. Appearance

   Children evaluate themselves by their reactions to their outward physical appearance. During the school years, the child's appearance and the way he or she dresses become crucial to the child's beliefs about himself or herself and his or her value. Peer pressure runs rampant!

2. Performance

   The child asks the question "How am I?" or, perhaps, "How do I compare with others, especially my peers?" The child learns early on that he or she lives in a competitive and work-oriented society.

   As children, most of us feel judged as either a success or a failure. Even for a child, self-image is closely tied to performance. The child who is constantly trying to please others (especially parents) might grow into adulthood to become a workaholic.

3. Importance

    The child asks, "How important am I?" One of the ways we determine how important we are to our parents is to gauge the amount of time they spend with us as a child. Does the child wait all day for Daddy to come home to sit upon his lap, but when Dad comes home, he reads the paper, watches TV, and then says good night to his child? This child would feel neglected, perhaps abandoned after a while, rejected, and certainly unimportant. All of us have formulated a mental image of ourselves based on the feeling of either acceptance or rejection we received from our parents.

Dr. Maurice Wagner, a Christian counselor, in his book *The Sensation of Being Somebody*, lists three essential components of a healthy self-image, as follows:

1. A sense of belonging and of being loved

    Wagner mentions that this is simply "an awareness of being wanted, accepted, cared for, enjoyed, and loved." He also states his belief that this starts before birth. An unwanted child will rarely have a sense of belonging.

2. A sense of worth and value

   This is described as an inner belief in ourselves. It is telling ourselves we are of value; "I count, and I have something to offer."

3. A sense of being competent

   This is a feeling that one can cope with the situation or can do the task at hand. How often a parent will tell his or her own child, "You will never amount to anything." This certainly does not do much to build up a sense of competence in the child! So often parents innocently hurt their own children! If a child is programmed for incompetence, then he or she will be incompetent.

Sources of Self-Image

In his classic book *Healing for Damaged Emotions*, David Seamands lists four sources of a person's self-image, as follows:

1. The outer world

   According to Seamands, this includes all the factors that have gone into our makeup, such as heredity;

experience in infancy, childhood, and the teenage years; and all of life's experiences right up to the present time. This primarily reflects the beliefs of our parents and other family members and the messages we received about ourselves. Such message may be transmitted to us not only in words, but also in facial expressions, attitudes, and actions when we are growing up. We can certainly trace this all the way back to Adam and Eve. They were not the image of perfect.

Before we go and blame everything on our parents, let us remember that we live in a fallen and imperfect world. Parents are imperfect as well. Most will do (and have done) the very best they know how as learned from their worldly parents; Through the first sin of Adam and Eve, a chain reaction was set in motion of imperfect parenting through failures, ignorance, misguided actions, and worst of all, conditional love. I wonder if Cain and Abel saw much conflict in their parents when they were children.

2. The inner world

   This is the world within us. This inner world includes our senses and our capacity to learn, register thoughts, and respond. This can also include handicaps and so-called physical or emotional defects. It should be added that the Bible makes it perfectly clear that we are not merely "victims" but are sinners, and we share in taking responsibility for who we are and who we are becoming.

3. Satan

   The third source of low self-esteem is directly from the pit of hell—Satan. There will not be any affirmation coming from this source. Instead, it is guaranteed that condemnation, accusations, and lies will be the flaming darts of the evil one. We are reminded through God's Word that Satan is a liar (John 8:44) and is the accuser (Revelation 12:10), and if we allow it, he will blind our minds (2 Corinthians 4:4). In all these roles, Satan will attack your self-image. You must not allow him to control your mind! That is where the battlefield is!

4. God

    This is to be the true source of our self-image. As David
    Seamands so beautifully states, to God is where we go
    to "turn away from the disease to its cure."

Some Effects of Poor Self-Image

The following are just a few of the more significant things that
befall us when we have a poor self-image. These are mentioned
at this time only so that the counselor may be aware of them.
It is not my intention to address the symptoms or treatment for
each of these categories.

Anxiety

One of the causes of anxiety is a low self-esteem and/or
poor self-image. Many people like to look good and perform
competently, and will feel threatened by anything that could
harm their self-image. Any such threat might bring anxiety
into their lives. A poor self-image can open the door to anxiety
attacks. On the contrary, a person with a healthy self-image
will have the confidence that he or she can meet the challenges

facing him or her. A healthy attitude is one that believes *There is nothing that God and I cannot handle this day!* This trust in God will go a long way toward fighting anxiety. People who suffer from anxiety are very gifted when it comes to their self-talk and misbeliefs! I say this tongue in cheek as these people are masters at believing Satan's lies about themselves or their situation.

The biggest lie is, "If the thing I'm worrying about actually happened, it would destroy me or wipe me out." Some other common lies and misbeliefs are as follows:

1. "He [or she] might not like me. That would be terrible!"
2. "I might not meet other people's expectations of me. That would be terrible!"
3. "I might be rejected. That would be terrible!"
4. "I might fail. That would be terrible!"
5. "I might say something stupid. That would be terrible!"
6. "Once he [or she] loves me, I might lose that love. How terrible!"
7. "I might lose everything I have! How terrible!"
8. "I could die. That would be terrible!"

The central theme running through the mind of this type of person is what other people may think of him or her. This is of prime and crucial importance! Nearly all anxious people believe they are in danger because of other people's reactions to them. This is a misbelief created by Satan himself.

The Bible does *not* teach that we have to please everyone we encounter on earth. Jesus was not (and still is not) loved and accepted by everyone. Jesus did not live to please people on earth; He lived to please His Father in heaven. No one other than you has the power to make you feel miserable. That power is yours alone.

Anxiety involves the following things:

1. fear in the absence of real danger
2. overestimation of the probability of danger and exaggeration of its degree of terribleness
3. imagined negative results.

The two major misbeliefs of a person with anxiety are as follows:

1. *If the thing I worry about were to happen, it would be terrible.*

2. *Even though the likelihood of the terrible thing happening to me is utterly remote, I believe it's actually inevitable.*

Most anxieties are related to one or more of the following four things:

1. dread (fear) of making a mistake in public
2. fear of making someone else angry or upset
3. loss of love
4. physical pain and/or death.

In reality, we, not situations or events, create anxiety. Anxiety is brought on by our telling ourselves that something is terrible. Another misbelief in action!

Following are two questions to ask yourself, and two answers:

1. "What am I telling myself is so terrible?"
   Response: "It's not terrible! It may be unpleasant, but that's a long way from terrible!"

2. "Will the results be as terrible as I am telling myself?"

Response: "Even if what I fear really were to happen, it would not be terrible. It might be unpleasant, but it surely will not be the end of me!"

The one thing *not* to do with anxiety is to avoid it! If you avoid anxiety, you will only increase the anxiety. If you face the anxiety and go through it, you will remove it! Rather than avoiding it, tell yourself, "Even though I'd like to avoid anxiety in all circumstances, I will not avoid it. This will only increase my anxiety. It may be unpleasant, but I will get through it with God. I do not have to be afraid of unpleasant feelings either. There's nothing that Jesus and I cannot go through together!"

To remove the anxiety, you have to face it. Then you have four more steps to go through, as follows:

1. Minimize the danger you tell yourself you are in. Fear brings on exaggeration.

2. Realize you create your own anxiety by your misbeliefs or believing Satan's lies.

3. Dispute and challenge these misbeliefs. Ask yourself, "Is this really as terrible as I'm telling myself?"

4. Replace the misbelief and Satan's lies with God's truth: "It is written …" Read 2 Corinthians 12:9 and be reminded that God is saying to you, "Each time he [God] said, 'My grace is all you need. My power works best in weakness, so that the power of Christ can work through me.'"

Loneliness

It is when we have a low opinion of ourselves that we will underestimate our self-worth. It is believed that when we have good self-esteem and a healthy self-image, we have confidence in ourselves to build relationships, which in turn will decrease the loneliness in our lives. On the flip side of this, poor self-image usually results in a tendency to feel weak, perhaps to feel shy, and to withdraw. The next stage of loneliness occurs when others are not there for us, at which point an extremely deep feeling of loneliness can set in. Failure in relationships can lower self-esteem and/or self-image and can be one of the causes of loneliness. As a person becomes lonelier, he or she withdraws into a self-centered feeling and sometimes self-pity and the "poor me" attitude. This is when the lie of Satan enters to tell you ethose things will never get better. The lonely cycle is perpetuated.

Depression

One of the many effects of depression is low self-image and self-esteem. When a person becomes discouraged and bored with life, this can also lead to self-pity and a lack of confidence. Although I do not intend to discuss the topic of depression at length, I do need to mention that as we help people become free of depression, we need to affirm them; help them change their self-image from the false one they have received from humans to one that God gives them; help them see themselves through God's eyes; and help them to understand that this is a process.

Anger

One of the ways we can help our counselees with anger problems is to help them build a healthy concept of themselves. Anger, as well as hostility, often indicates that a person feels inferior compared to others. Often this type of person will react with anger when someone attempts to assert authority. This certainly seems to be happening in our inner cities with our youth when confronted with those in authority. It has been said that the stronger our self-concept becomes, the easier it is for us to manage anger. Anger can be less destructive and more easily controlled when a person is secure in himself or herself and not plagued by feelings of inferiority, a poor self-image, and low self-esteem. When Christians have a realistic picture of themselves as God sees them, they feel less of a need or inclination to become angry.

Guilt

Many causes of guilt are tied to our self-esteem and self-image. I will not attempt at this time to discuss the difference between true guilt and false guilt. Often true guilt is easier to deal with by taking this sin of guilt to the cross and allowing the blood of Jesus to wash and cleanse us of the guilt we have been carrying. It is false guilt that we tend to carry when we have an unhealthy self-image.

Old Age

This is not to imply that with a healthy self-image, we will not grow old! Please do not misunderstand me. The point I wish to make is that too often people in their golden years have a low self-image (I should know—I am at this stage of life at ninety-one years young). Our self-confidence and self-esteem is undermined by our self-talk and also by what we hear from others. I believe it is important for the elderly to have and maintain a healthy self-image. Our children, grandchildren, friends, and church community need to confirm how God sees us.

Adultery

As strange as it may seem, one of the causes of sex outside of marriage is a person's self-image and self-esteem. Again, do not misunderstand me: this is not an excuse for adultery! Sex outside marriage does occur at times when one partner is suffering from low self-image and/or low self-esteem. Someone who fits this description may use adultery to prove his or her self-image to himself or herself.

Alcoholism

Many alcoholics have high anxiety, low self-esteem, and/or a poor self-image.

Addictions.

The effect of other addictions is the same as the effect of alcoholism. Low self-esteem and poor self-image often enter the scene and need to be dealt. These arise because the individual is unable to meet excessively high standards and, as a result, feels worthless, unlovable, and like a failure. In addition, such a person cannot understand why God would love him or her.

The Continuing Development of Self-Worth

Self-image is mainly established by the authority figures to whom we are in submission in childhood. This is how we learn who we are. Our everyday experiences from childhood shape our self-image. We need to keep in mind that the general atmosphere in our families will contribute to our view of ourselves more than any single event. Is it now understandable how crucial it is to raise children in a safe and affirming environment?

There are several characteristics of a family that build self-esteem into the children, as follows:

- An attitude of unconditional love and acceptance
  This is the most important!

- An attitude of understanding

  In order to be understood, children need to express their feelings and be taught that these feelings are valid. If the child "stuffs" his or her feelings because he or she is not permitted to express them, he or she will feel unaccepted.

- Flexibility of the parents in the family

  Parents, avoid being so rigid that your children dare not step out of line. However, it is crucial to maintain boundaries and to discipline your children. Balance is needed.

Three ingredients for God's strategy for parenting are as follows:

1. Modeling

   Parents are to serve as positive role models for their children. Children will observe their parents and even imitate them in words, behavior, and attitude. It is from our parents that we establish our worldly belief systems. The Old Testament family structure would be a good model to resurrect today. We need to move from the so-called "nuclear family" to the "kingdom family." Perhaps "covenant family" would be a better name to call this latter type. In this type of family, the parents are respected and looked up to. When the temple in Jerusalem was destroyed, each family became a "miniature temple" and the family became a house of prayer. The dinner table became *the altar*, where eating was not just a physical exercise but a spiritual event ("One does not live by bread alone"). What models do we need to reestablish? Ephesians 6:4 calls us to be good role models for our children. We are not to exasperate our children, but we are called to be sensitive role models of maturity, stability, and peace for our children.

2. Teaching

Parents are to teach their children godly principles for living. This includes verbal teaching as well as discipline. The Old Testament teachings were solidly emphasized to Jesus as He was growing up as a child.

The well-known Holy Scriptures from Deuteronomy 11:19 emphasize the importance of teaching biblical principles to our children: "Teach them to your children, talking about them when you sit at home and when you walk along the road, when you lie down and when you get up." In other words, do it all the time! Do not stop! There are similar passages in the fourth chapter of Deuteronomy and in Exodus. Since God has repeated these instructions about teaching His Word to our children, we must regard it as extremely important.

3. Learning to Relate

Parents are to relate to their children in a loving and affirming way. Learning to relate is crucial. If there is no warm and loving relationship between parent and child, then the other two ingredients, modeling and teaching, will be ineffective. As mentioned previously, this bonding and healthy relationship should start when the child is in the womb. The child needs to understand that it is wanted, desired, and loved.

A child's development involves three stages of parental influence. Although it is important for the child to have *both* parents involved in his or her developmental nurturing, it is also important to recognize these three influential stages. It is also noteworthy to mention that many children grow up beautifully with just one nurturing parent. However, there is usually someone else who fills one of the nurturing roles, such as an uncle, a grandparent, or even a peer. Also, remember that the pregnancy stage is important as the child can be nurtured by way of voice from both parents during this time!

Following are three needs that must be met in order for a child to develop in a healthy way:

1. The need to feel loved and accepted and to have a sense of belonging

    When we were born, we had no self-image. This developed slowly in us as we took in the data, attitudes, and atmosphere around us. A good self-image comes from the quality of relationships between us and those who played significant roles in our early lives. God's plan or blueprint is for parents to be godly gifts to their children no matter how they may feel about the unconditional love and acceptance they themselves received, or failed to receive, growing up. We can absorb into our spirit the thought, *The One who knows me the best is the One who loves me the most.* This certainly is a love that we do not deserve or could ever earn! It has been demonstrated to us by our heavenly Father sending His one and only Son to die for us so that we will never perish but have eternal life!

Along with His unconditional love comes His unconditional acceptance. We cannot earn His acceptance through good deeds or performance. He accepts us through His unconditional love and accepts us *just as we are.* Even though we make mistakes and fall into sin, He is still there. However, He allows the consequences of our sins to teach us as He applies His loving discipline and/or chastisement. As we learn the fact that God loves us, we can begin to become motivated to accept ourselves. This door to self-acceptance will open after we comprehend God's acceptance of us—again, just as we are. This sets us free so that we can be. We need to be constantly reminded of the scripture in Romans 15:7: "Accept one another just as Christ accepted you, in order to bring praises to God." This acceptance is a must for the body of Christ—the church.

2. The need to feel worthy through acceptance

As we relate to being accepted, we begin to acquire a sense of worthiness. We begin to like ourselves as any shame that is present start its process of melting away. Our sense of our worthiness rests with God the Son. Even if we think we have flunked the test of life, our Lord Jesus can and will forgive us everything if we ask Him and repent. We have been made worthy, worthy enough even to be forgiven of all our sins and shortcomings. Even when we miss the mark, God has made us worthy to be forgiven! First John 1:9 needs to be engraved into our minds and spirits: "If we confess our sins, He is faithful and just and will forgive us our sins and purify us from all unrighteousness."

Let us also never forget Paul's words found in Romans 8:1: "Therefore, there is now no condemnation for those who are in Christ Jesus." God may "convict" us, but He does not condemn us. If we are victims of condemnation, be clear that the condemnation is from the depths of hell and not from our Lord.

The most difficult act of forgiveness is to forgive ourselves. It is much easier to forgive others. We are so hard on ourselves! It is through forgiveness of others, and forgiving of ourselves especially, that our healthy self-image can be released so as to flow into setting us free to be. It has been said that if we cannot forgive ourselves, we are really telling Jesus that He died on the cross for others perhaps, but not for us. We are negating the cross! As I have heard our friend David Seamands say, "A friend of mine who is a psychiatrist has said if his patients could understand and receive forgiveness, 'I would lose half my patients.'" I also recall something Martin Luther wrote: "God does not love us because we are valuable; we are valuable because God loves us."

How awesome! We are worthy through being created by God, and we have a greater worthiness because of the cross of Jesus Christ and His unconditional love for each one of us. We are worthy because of our creation and our Creator, and the redemption made possible by the shedding of Jesus's blood.

3. The need to have a sense of competence

   A sense that we are competent will give us an optimistic outlook on life and on ourselves. Our sense of competence rests with God the Holy Spirit. As we come to understand and experience our relationship with the Holy Spirit, our confidence is rebuilt and restored. This can get us from the despairing or hopeless stage to the stage of hope in our lives. (*Note:* This is very important in counseling as there will be times when your only job is to get a counselee out of despair. This will give them new life by giving encouragement through hope in their circumstances).

The Bible gives us insight into our relationship with the Holy Spirit. We have been born of the Spirit (John 3:3–5); the Spirit lives within us (John 14:17); the Spirit will be with us forever (John 14:16); the Holy Spirit teaches us all we need to know (John 14:26); the Spirit testifies to us that we are children of God (Romans 8:16); He guides us (Romans 8:14); He provides us with talents and gifts as He determines (1 Corinthians 12:4); He helps us in our weakness and intercedes for us (Romans 8:26–27); and He develops us as we mature with the fruits of the Spirit (Galatians 5:22–23). The Christian life can only be lived by the power of the Holy Spirit! As you might have concluded from the foregoing, as we grow in and with the Spirit, our confidence and our competence will grow into maturity. And yet, when we receive the Holy Spirit into our lives, we have *everything we will ever need*. What a glorious promise from God!

However, there are three things needed to prepare for the Holy Spirit's in-filling, as follows:

1. We must have a hunger and a thirst for God and be open to His Spirit. We cannot ask God to limit His Spirit upon us, either. Too often, we attempt to tell God what part of the Spirit or what gifts we want to receive. We

have to be open and willing for whatever God wants to give us and do in our lives.

2. We must be willing to submit and surrender the control of our lives to the Holy Spirit. Too often in the secular realm, we think of the word *surrender* in negative terms (e.g., "It is not macho to surrender!"). In the military, it is evil just to think of this word. In God's eyes and language, to surrender is to become victorious. He desires us to surrender to Him with no strings attached. By faith we know He will not lead us astray. Give *all* of yourself to Him. You cannot reach for the brass ring until you surrender and get on the carousel.

3. We need to cleanse ourselves by confessing all known sins in our lives. We ask God to forgive us of all sins, known and unknown. Then, by faith in God's Word, we *know* that we have been cleansed and purified by the atoning blood of Jesus. Parents can play an important role in this development stage of their children. As parents, we need to encourage our children to take risks, to explore and venture out away from Mom and Dad. The child who grows up with a sheltered life

and is not allowed to take risks may mature with an underdeveloped sense of competence and confidence. This may restrict him or her from becoming free to be. People with this underdeveloped sense of competence may strive for perfection, which can be bondage in and of itself. They might become workaholics with the false notion that if only they accomplish enough, they will be worthy of people's love.

After we've accomplished the foregoing three goals, we need to study Holy Scripture to learn of the lifestyles of the people God has used for His glory. Many times throughout history we find that the people whom God used were those who had surrendered to Him. After surrendering and allowing God to work in their lives, our Lord took their weaknesses or limitations and turned them into strengths. When we learn of our weaknesses and confess them, our Lord might convict us to rely upon Him to overcome those weaknesses and turn them into strengths. Remember Paul's confession in 2 Corinthians 12:9 when he was struggling with the thorn in his flesh. God's response was, "My grace is sufficient for you, for My power is made perfect in weakness."

Moses may be a good example to look at as well. When Moses was growing up in Pharaoh's court, he was useful, was strong, and had a sphere of influence on others. However, he was of no use to God. When Moses was useless and living in the desert as a nomad, God could finally use him for His glory.

Never Taking a Chance

Some of our misbeliefs keep us from ever taking a chance in life. This thought can be devastating to many people. We need to know that it is *not* wisdom that causes us to refuse to take a risk; it is *fear* that presents us with the greatest threat to our doing so. A partial list of misbeliefs that keep a person from taking chances is as follows:

1. "I need to prevent any way of getting hurt."
2. "Taking a chance could lead to a calamity or disaster in my life."
3. "Being safe is of utmost importance; it is terrible to be in danger."
4. "It is terrible to make a wrong decision."

5. "If I take a chance, I could lose everything!"

6. "I don't dare make mistakes; mistakes are terrible."

7. "God does not approve of taking risks and certainly does not bless our mistakes."

8. "Taking a risk could lead to someone's rejecting me."

9. "It is sinful to make a mistake."

Let's look at the greatest risk ever taken. God Himself took the greatest risk of a great loss when He set out to build His kingdom here on earth. He sent His one and only Son, Jesus Christ, to earth for our sake. When Jesus started His ministry, He took the chance of losing His reputation, His family, His security, His home, and His popularity—all for the sake of His heavenly Father!

God certainly took a great risk when He created us with a free will. Even with His having giving us our free will, our prerogative to choose life or death, and even permission to rebel against Him, He was still willing to take this chance with us.

Risk-taking is part of human life. Consider the following statements:

1. We cannot lead a happy, peaceful life without taking risks.

2. To gain a friend, we take a chance of being rejected.

3. To speak up and be heard by others, we risk being corrected.

4. To be noticed, we take a chance of being ignored.

5. To get a job, we risk being turned down.

6. To win, we risk defeat.

7. Faith itself is a risk.

It is to be hoped we know that the Christian walking by the Holy Spirit in the will of God can trust that the outcomes of his or her actions in faith are totally in the hands of the Father.

Every time a misbelief or lie enters our thought lives, we are compelled to recognize it as a misbelief and argue against it. Then we should replace it with God's truth and confess that Jesus Christ is Lord over our lives.

The purpose of risk-taking is as follows:

1. To teach us to seek the Lord for His will in all situations in which we have felt fear.

2. To trust our Lord to act on our behalf according to His will.

3. To obey our Lord by following His directives for action.

4. To experience our Lord's blessings by working through our anxieties with Him.

> By working through these four progressive steps, we learn that by actually doing the thing we fear, we will actually overcome the fear!

A Testimony of Being Freed from Misbeliefs and a Poor Self-Image

I received a testimonial letter from a Christian friend in South Carolina who was set free from the bondage of misbelief. When she learned of my desire to write on this topic, her comment was, "Amid all the fast-moving stuff, God continues his marvelous healing in my life, little by little, at His pace. I am truly transformed from years ago, and His mercies are new every morning. I love the concept of your proposed [book] title, *Free to Be*, since learning to *be* instead of *doing* all the time has been so central in my journey to wholeness."

As you hear this story of God's healing power, also keep in mind the four steps to healing misbeliefs:

1. Identify the lie or misbelief.
2. Recognize the misbeliefs and renounce them as lies in contradiction of God's Word. Ask God to forgive you for believing these lies, which surely hurts Him. Prayers for forgiveness are necessary. When you deny your identity, your gifts, and your talents as gifts that come from God, you are actually in *rebellion* against God. You are saying to God that you are not pleased with the way He created you and gifted you. How wonderful it is to know He will indeed forgive you when you go to Him with repentance in your heart!
3. Argue against the misbelief through the wisdom and power of the Holy Spirit—the Spirit of truth.
4. Replace the misbelief or Satan's lies with God's truth about you and/or the situation.

The Testimony

Our friend was diagnosed with clinical depression. The depression was being treated primarily with medications to improve how she felt. At no time was there any effort to arrive at the source of the depression, as the thrust was to have her feel better. She had visited her pastor for prayer help, and he had told her she was a basket case!

Her spiritual journey was solid. Her parents are strong Christian believers, and she was active in a renewed Spirit-filled church. She knows Jesus as her Lord and Savior and has a deep prayer life. Her husband, too, is a strong believer and is the spiritual head of the home. They are both aware of the power of Satan's lies; moreover they know the Word of God, which has power *and* authority over the evil one.

This woman had come to visit my wife Anne and me for prayer. The three of us started in prayer and asked for the guidance, wisdom, and power of the Holy Spirit. We asked for God to guide us to learn the root cause of the woman's depression. What was astonishing to us (surely not to God!) was that God gave each one of us a word of knowledge, all of which tied together. Anne received from the Spirit the word *school*; I received the words that the depression had started in early childhood around the age of five to six; and God was right on with our counselee as she came up with the word *kindergarten*.

Her memory of her kindergarten graduation came into her mind. She shared with us that on her graduation day, with the room full of parents, the teacher had asked many questions to the class to show the parents how much the children had learned. This woman recalled that the children were instructed to raise their hands when they knew the answers.

She had raised her hand to every question; she knew all the answers! Finally, the teacher asked the class, "Does anyone else know any of the answers?" When our friend's classmates and the parents laughed, her belief system kicked into high gear. The misbelief that she had told herself, one that had continued to haunt her even into adult life, was, "It's too embarrassing to be smart, and it's much safer to pretend to be dumb. I'd better stop raising my hand in class!" She shared that as this became a family joke, she became even more embarrassed. Soon she told herself the misbelief "I'm not supposed to know any answers to questions."

Also in the session, our friend remembered that in the second grade she got into trouble because she would do none of the work. She even shared that she remembered that at the end of second grade, there were only two pieces of finished schoolwork in her folder! The next misbelief she told herself was, "I need to make sure that I am not good enough." Throughout her education years, she was haunted with the misbelief (part of Satan's bombardment of lies) "I am not good as a student; as a matter of fact, I am not good at anything!" This misbelief has haunted her into adult life, as she still had been telling herself another, similar misbelief: "I am not smart enough; I am surely going to get fired." Because of this misbelief, she had difficulty holding a job.

This is a prime example that we really do not go out to dig up the past, but we do need to learn the source of the misbeliefs we have told ourselves. God wants us to be set free of these bondages, and He is faithful to us.

With the misbeliefs exposed and identified by the Holy Spirit, the next steps are to remove the misbeliefs and replace them with *the truth*.

The three of us prayed for God to remove the lies from our friend's mind and her thought patterns. We also led her in a prayer of forgiveness. This is crucial to all healing as we need to ask our Lord to forgive us for denying ourselves. It is a form of rebellion when we deny our lives and gifts as the very lives and gifts that God has given to us. God in His infinite wisdom also reminded our friend of the parable of the talents in Matthew 25:14–30. This parable was told by Jesus more than two thousand years ago, but it was speaking to our friend now! She exclaimed rather loudly, "God just spoke to me and said I buried my God-given talent!" She was in tears and humbly asked her Lord to forgive her for burying this talent. She also asked for forgiveness for desiring mediocrity, as she said she did not want to succeed yet did not want to fail.

We read this scripture together and were awestruck upon reading God's sentence for the servant who had buried his talent. Scripture refers to the master throwing this servant "out into the darkness, where there will be weeping and gnashing of teeth." We agreed that this certainly sounded a lot like depression to us!

Our friend felt such a release of God's love, joy, and peace at this time. We heard from her a short time after her visit and learned that she had been released from her psychologist and had been taken off all medication for the depression.

God's therapeutic weapon is *truth*. God's truth will indeed set us free! This testimony illustrates how one person was set free from the misbeliefs of the past, and how God desires His children to be set free. Yes, we are free to be! Praise our Lord!

Surrender!

The word, *surrender* has different meanings for different people. For some, surrender is something to be avoided at all costs. For some, this is the most difficult stumbling block. Some even think, If *I surrender all of me, I will become a prisoner of war!* Frankly, it's just the opposite. I remember a general once said, "We will *never* surrender or retreat! We will only do an about-face and advance!" To our God, this word *surrender* means total victory. What a difference! I believe Jesus our Messiah calls us to one thing: *to surrender to Him.* That is the only event that leads to victory. Many Christians attempt to bargain with God to set the terms for surrender. He will not surrender on our terms; we need to get that clear in our heads and hearts! God will accept our surrender only on His terms! Do you ever tell God "I'll surrender to You *if* You will do certain things for me?"

So often we see this in the ministry of healing. We ask

God to heal us of our infirmities or heal some emotional or spiritual problem we are struggling with. Sometimes He asks us to look at the sin in our lives first. God says, *Surrender to Me first.* God says to seek first His kingdom and that all these other things will fall into place (Matthew 6:33). It is only through total surrender that we can enter through the doorway to kingdom living.

Let's see what the dictionary says about surrender: "to relinquish possession or control to another because of demand or force." This doesn't quite fit with God's definition, as our Lord will not force Himself upon us. However, He does call us to give up our control to Him. He also compels us to give up our control of others to Him.

Let's not confuse surrender for commitment. We really can commit to something or someone without surrendering. We can commit to giving a relationship a couple of years to see if it will ultimately work out. We can commit to a job until something better comes along. To surrender means to give all of you to the project. To surrender in God's kingdom is to give up *anything* God asks you to give up and to receive *everything* He desires to give you. I believe that without total surrender to God, we will struggle to find our total freedom to be.

One of the most compelling books I have ever read is Jan David Hettinga's *Follow Me*. It is about the call that Jesus places upon our lives to follow Him as His disciple. It was through my reading of this book that the word *surrender* became a sign of victory for me. The author uses one sentence to sum up the entire gospel message of Jesus: "The heart of the Christian gospel is Jesus's offer to be the leader we can trust and His insistence that every believer become a follower He can trust!"

The sheer honesty of Jesus is displayed. He tells us what we may expect if we choose to follow Him. He is saying, "If you choose to follow Me, I need to be number one in your life." Another way to look at this is to believe that in order to receive His presents (gifts of the Holy Spirit), you need to be in His presence. The author of *Follow Me* further states that the bridge from the kingdom of self to the kingdom of God is built through true repentance—turning away from sin and latching onto something else (such as God), that is, repenting from the heart. Is there anything keeping you from kingdom living now? What among those things that you need to surrender is

God stirring your heart toward? Is there sin that still controls you? Do you have any other stumbling blocks to place at the foot of the cross? As a side note, I believe in praying to our infallible loving Father. I also personally believe, as evidenced by my own journey, that it always pleases God when we confess openly and personally to a fellow believer whom we trust and love. I believe God desires one word from us as He calls us: "Yes!" He seeks our yes and calls for our total surrender to Him. Not "Maybe" or "I'm waiting for a sign from You first." The first step to total surrender is up to us!

A teaching I used to share is a tool I used to explain the old tradition of a leader who has surrendered his troops to a conqueror giving up his saber or sword by handing it over to the victor. There are numerous old expressions of this tradition even in our nation. I also am reminded of the statement Jesus made about the sword in Matthew 10:34: "Don't imagine that I came to bring peace to the earth! I came not to bring peace, but a sword."

The sword handed over is a sign of surrender. Throughout military history, the conqueror was to receive the sword of the defeated enemy. Many times, the victor would break the sword of his defeated foe. Here are a few examples from history:

When Emperor Napoleon Bonaparte was defeated, he allowed shame to overcome him. He was so ashamed that he could not hand his sword to his conqueror. Legend has it that it was Desiree who approached Napoleon and offered to accept his sword and turn it over to his victors. Supposedly this allowed him to avoid shame.

At the conclusion of the Revolutionary War on these shores, the surrender of the British troops took place at Yorktown in October 1781. Article 3 of the terms of surrender states the following: "The English garrison to march out at three o'clock in the afternoon, the cavalry with their swords drawn, trumpets sounding, and the infantry in the manner prescribed for the garrison of York." The drawn sword was a sign of total surrender. It is interesting to learn that Lord Charles Cornwallis, unwilling to humiliate himself, refused to meet General Washington. Instead, he sent a surrogate officer with Cornwallis's sword to demonstrate the surrender in full. Like Napoleon, Cornwallis also suffered from an overdose of pride and perhaps shame. Some history texts assert that he was too ill to attend the surrender ceremony. Just like Lord Cornwallis and Napoleon, many of us, I believe, are unable to completely surrender to God because we first must conquer shame and/or pride. Through prayer and asking God to forgive us of these two sins, we can be totally set free to be!

I recently heard a fascinating story about the Russian hero Ivan the Great. It seemed he needed to find a wife in order to raise up a czar. In order to have royalty in the bloodline, Sophia, a niece of the king of Greece, was selected for his bride. The Greek Orthodox Church required that Ivan be baptized in the Mediterranean Sea. As he was being immersed in the water, he raised his forearm with his hand clutching his sword so that the sword would not go under the water. He could go through the ritual, but he would not surrender all.

There are two more quick stories to tell. One is the surrender of Robert E. Lee to General Ulysses S. Grant at the conclusion of the Civil War at Appomattox, Virginia. Legend has it that after Lee humbly gave his sword to General Grant as a sign of surrender, Grant graciously returned it to him as a sign of his honoring him as a great adversary.

One great event in my childhood that I still remember is

the total surrender of the Japanese nation to the United States. This took place aboard the battleship USS *Missouri* in Tokyo harbor in 1945. Let's set the scene: All the dignitaries were present aboard ship, including General Wainwright, who had been captured in the Philippines when the war began. Also representing our nation was General Douglas MacArthur. When it came to the actual signing of the documents and surrender, the Japanese admiral extended his hand to MacArthur as a sign of friendship and peace. General MacArthur kept his own hand at his side and refused to shake hands with the admiral. Sternly, he said, *"Sir, your sword first, please."* Only after the sword had been handed over to MacArthur would he take the hand of the defeated Japanese admiral. MacArthur knew that the sword was a symbol of formal surrender and disarming of the enemy.

The following is a powerful and touching hymn that was birthed in 1896 and is still sung in many churches today. Let it soak into your spirit as you read the lyrics. The prospect of actually surrendering all can be a stumbling block for some. However, with the power of the Holy Spirit, you have the power to turn your surrender into a mere stepping-stone. Go for it!

I Surrender All

All to Jesus I surrender,
all to Him I freely give;
I will ever love and trust Him,
in His presence daily live.

I surrender all.
I surrender all;
all to thee, my blessed Savior,
I surrender all.
All to Jesus I surrender.
Humbly at His feet I bow,
Worldly pleasures all forsaken.
Take me, Jesus. Take me now.
All to Jesus I surrender.
Make me, Savior, wholly thine.
Let me feel the Holy Spirit,
truly know that thou art mine.
All to Jesus I surrender.
Lord, I give myself to thee.
Fill me with thy love and power,
let thy blessing fall on me.
All to Jesus I surrender.
Now I feel the sacred flame;
Oh, the joy of full salvation!
Glory, glory, to His name!
(Lyrics by Judson W. VanDeVenter, 1896; music by
Winfield S. Weeden, 1896)

Ponder Page

1. Reread Ephesians 3:16–19. Allow the phrase "as you trust in Him" to manifest in your mind. Where is your trust level? If not at 100 percent, what can you do to increase your level of trust in God?

2. As an assignment, google Eden's Bridge rendition of "I Will Change Your Name." Then ask God to give you a new name if He so desires.

3. Through prayer. Ask God if you are still holding on to any unforgiveness. If so, then give this unforgiveness to God.

4. Put a name on your "sword" (such as fear, shame, guilt, or abandonment) and surrender it to God. What does the word *surrender* mean to you? Do you see victory in total surrender?

5. Explain how one can be in total freedom by giving up total control to God.

6. Can you relate to the scripture James 4:7–8, where it says to resist the devil and he will flee from you; to come close to God and He will come close to you?

7. Do you believe in the free gift of God's grace and the freedom He offers?

Chapter 3

Building the Foundation

To review, let us recall the three basic emotional needs we all have:

1. the need to feel loved and accepted and to have a sense of belonging,

2. the need to feel acceptable and have a sense of being worthy, and

3. the need to feel adequate and have a sense of competence.

It is in these three areas that the foundation of our self-image is built. It is through our journey in our relationship with our heavenly Father that we come to see ourselves the way He sees us. This is the beginning of our journey to form a healthy image of ourselves, and similar to other journeys, this one begins with the very first step. Following is an accurate account of our walk with our Lord into wholeness. Keep in mind that this is a journey and a process. It usually does not happen quickly, yet God can do whatever He desires to do. From my experience as a counselor and prayer minister, I believe that the more wounded an individual has been, especially by the very people who were supposed to be his or her primary caregivers, the longer it will take for the process of ultimately healing his or her self-image to be completed. On the contrary, those of us who have grown up being affirmed, loved, and accepted, and instilled with a sense of belonging, do not have a struggle with self-image. (*Note:* Even though I grew up in this type of loving atmosphere, I can attest to the fact that Satan will always put people in our paths who will attempt to destroy our self-image or call it into question.)

The truth of who we are is to come from Holy Scripture. Even as the wounded counselees begin to understand this, they will comment, "The Word of God might be okay for someone else, but it could not possibly be for me." This is another one of Satan's lies and traps (or snares) that conveniently placed in our roadway. Josh McDowell, author of *His Image, My Image*, uses the analogy of a pilot flying by using only instruments. This is easy for me to relate to because of my experience with flying and receiving my instrument rating as a pilot. It is very easy to attempt to determine the position and altitude of the airplane based on how one feels. At the beginning, a pilot's feelings are used to determine how the airplane is reacting. After some hours of instruction, you finally begin to ignore the feelings and to rely only upon what the instruments tell you! This is exactly what we must do as we begin to fly into freedom with God. We need to prevent relying on how it feels. The Word of God must be our instrument panel. What does God's Word say about us? about me? about you? We *must* correct any faulty theology we have; only God's Word will correct any false beliefs we have been carrying. We cannot think wrongly and live rightly at the same time!

Forgiveness is a good example I can use to illustrate my meaning here. When we sin, we feel that God could not possibly forgive us for what we have done. However, what does the Word of God tell us about being forgiven?

First John 1:9, which reads, "If we confess our sins, He is faithful and just to forgive us our sins and to cleanse us from all unrighteousness," should be memorized and understood by every Christian! Our sense of our value and self-worth *has* to come from God, not from some false reflection from our past and surely not from Satan's lies. This decision to confess our sins must be made by us if we are to begin the process of healing of our self-image.

The Character of God

To understand the truth of who we are in God's eyes, we need to be sure we understand the character of our God. There are too many of us still living with a false image of God. We see God as a tyrant, a punishing taskmaster, or "a gotcha" kind of God who is waiting in the wings of our lives and watching for us to make a mistake.

In J. B. Phillips's classic book *Your God Is Too Small*, there is a list of the many false characterizations of God that many of us hold onto, as follows:

1. God the resident policeman
2. God-in-the-box
3. God the parental hangover (author's note: "parental headache")
4. God the managing director
5. God the grand old man

6. The secondhand God

7. God the meek and mild

8. God the perennial grievance committee

9. God the absolute perfectionist

10. The God for the elite only

11. God the heavenly bosom.

God's True Character

1. God is King of the universe (Psalm 24:8; 1 Chronicles 29:11–12; 2 Chronicles 20:6).

2. God is righteous (Psalm 119:137).

3. God is just (Deuteronomy 32:4).

4. God is love (1 John 4:8).

5. God is eternal (Deuteronomy 33:27).

6. God is all-knowing (2 Chronicles 16:9; Psalm 139:1–6).

7. God is everywhere (Psalm 139:7–10).

8. God is all-powerful (Job 42:2).

9. God is truth (Psalm 31:5).

10. God is unchangeable (Malachi 3:6).

11. God is faithful (Romans 15:5; Exodus 34:6).

12. God is holy (Revelation 15:4).

Who We Are in Jesus Christ

To learn who we are in Christ, we turn to Paul's Epistle to the Ephesians, chapters 1 and 2. This will help us to see ourselves as God sees us.

In chapter 1, we read the following:

1. We are blessed with every spiritual blessing in the heavenly places (verse 3).

2. We were chosen before the foundations of the world that we should be holy and blameless before Him (verse 4).

3. We are predestined to adoption as sons and daughters of God (verse 5).

4. We are redeemed through His blood (verse 7).

5. We are sealed in Him with the Holy Spirit (verse 13).

Additional truths that become evident to believers after we trust in Jesus Christ are described in Ephesians 2:4–10, as follows:

1. We are alive together in Christ.

2. We are raised with Christ.

3. We will be seated with Him in the heavenly places.

4. We are in Christ Jesus.

5. We are saved by grace.

6. We are made in His workmanship.

God Desires Us to Feel Secure, Significant, and Free

Holy Scripture is clear on the point that it is our God's desire that we feel worthy, significant, and secure and have a healthy self-image. First John 3:1 reminds us that God calls us "children of God." When a person is loved, he or she feels emotionally secure. God constantly reminds us of His love for us. It is important to remember that He calls us "children of God." This indicates that God wants us to realize that we are significant!

God continues to compliment us and affirm us by calling us "saints" (see Ephesians 1:1). He also calls us "heirs of God and fellow heirs with Christ" (Romans 8:17). We are also called "sons" (and daughters) of God (see Galatians 4:5–6), and we are "citizens of heaven" (Philippians 3:20). What an honor He has imposed upon us! By His grace, *we are worthy and significant*!

It should be added at this point that God really does *not* want us to pursue significance, self-worth, or a healthy self-image. His desire is for us to *pursue Him*! As we pursue Him, the rest will fall into place.

An image that has helped me is found in the well-known verse Revelation 3:20: "Look! I stand at the door and knock. If you hear my voice and open the door, I will come in, and we will share a meal together as friends." This is the story of Jesus standing at the door and knocking, desiring to come inside. This is a picture for believers. Jesus desires that we invite Him to dine with us. We are to invite Jesus into our mealtimes. This should be a time for fellowship and sharing among family members and guests. By this request, Jesus wants us to enjoy His company and to get to know Him better and become closer to Him. As we fellowship with Him, we feel that security, love, and acceptance more and more!

Anne and I saw a certain famous painting when we visited Saint Paul's Cathedral in London years ago. Our tour guide emphasized that the argument of the painting was directed toward believers in the church of Laodicea who had become lukewarm and in need of repentance. Also, it was no accident that the painter, William Hunt, included no door handle on the outside of the door: the door can be opened only by the persons on the inside! This describes me from time to time in the past—a person on the outside. Does it also describe you on your journey as a believer?

In order to feel secure with and significant to Jesus, we need to spend more time in this fellowship. It involves more than just soaking in His love. It also means to be obedient to Him who loves us. I believe when we fail to be obedient, we lose some of this sense of security. It is perfect love from God that "casts out fear," as mentioned in 1 John 4:18. When we are able to receive His perfect love for us, we can then feel secure in Him. In this security, we then realize our true self-image, which replaces whatever image we think we have based on Satan's lies.

Reminders of Who We Are in Christ Jesus

We need reminders of who we are in the eyes of our Lord Jesus Christ. We also need to remember that we are constantly engaged in spiritual warfare. Satan, who does not want us to know who we are in God's eyes, will continue to bombard us with his lies, accusations, and deceit. Let us never yield to the lies! We also need to remember that if we listen to lies long enough, we will become confused and may even begin to believe the lies. This was one of the secrets to the success of Adolf Hitler more than sixty years ago. He knew that if he lied long enough, the German people would begin to believe the lies—and indeed those lies became "the truth." (Read Isaiah 5:10.)

The following quotations from the Word of God need to be engraved or etched onto our minds, hearts, and souls:

1. "I have peace with God" (Romans 5:1).
2. "I am accepted by God" (Ephesians 1).
3. "I am a child of God" (John 1:12).
4. "I am indwelt by the Holy Spirit" (1 Corinthians 3:16).
5. "I have access to God's wisdom" (James 1:5).
6. "I am helped by God" (Hebrews 4:16).
7. "I am reconciled to God" (Romans 5:11).
8. "I have *no* condemnation" (Romans 8:1).
9. "I am justified" (Romans 5:1).

10. "I have His righteousness" (Romans 5:19; 2 Corinthians 5:21).

11. "I am His representative" (2 Corinthians 5:20).

12. "I am *completely* forgiven!" (Colossians 1:14; 1 John 1:9).

13. "I have my needs met by God" (Philippians 4:19).

14. "I am the aroma of Christ to God" (2 Corinthians 2:15).

15. "I am a temple of God" (1 Corinthians 3:16).

16. "I am blameless and beyond reproach" (Colossians 1:22).

I suggest to you that you continue to read Holy Scripture to find other quotations and references that speak to you as you move along in your own personal journey. There are too many to mention, and God speaks to each of us according to just where we are in our journey with Him. Romans 8:28 is another scripture that reminds me of God's love for us: "We know that in all things God works for the good of those who love Him, who have been called according to His purpose."

A healthy self-image is created by being committed to the truth of God's estimation of oneself. Let none of us ever be robbed of this again!

Reparenting: How It Can Heal a Poor Self-Image

We will look into reparenting and how it can be a useful tool to heal those with a damaged self-image. This is something I feel very strongly about as I have been a witness to God's healing power through reparenting.

The body of Christ, the church, is called to play a major role in reparenting. There are several approaches to reparenting. One method I will mention just briefly. It is for those who have been wounded in the past by their own parents. As we have discussed, many people grew up in a dysfunctional family and had a poor male role model or perhaps a poor model of what a woman's role in the family should be.

In my many years of ministry, I have been a (and I still submit to the role of) "spiritual dad" for many people. Also, I believe that the church calls some of us to play such a role for other members of the body of Christ. I strongly believe this can be a mission of many men's groups that serve only a social-type function in the church. Wouldn't it be glorious if these men would become spiritual fatherly advisers for young men or teenaged boys who need someone with whom to talk?

God's plan for the healing of a damaged self-image is patterned after His original parenting process. There are three major elements to this process:

- Modeling

  Healthy modeling is to come from the child's parents as by example.

- Teaching

  Teaching is also to come through the parents. This is to include discipline as well as the teaching process. We have previously discussed the Old Testament principle of God's calling parents to diligently teach their children almost "day and night." In other words, this kind of teaching involves much more than just the few hours per day that a child goes to school; it is an ongoing process of teaching—"when walking, sitting, lying down, and sitting up."

- Learning

  The learning process is another ongoing procedure that never stops. This is also to continue amid the atmosphere of the church. There is something to be learned from the early church in regard to God's design for transformation of one's self-image. God implemented a procedure for creating a good, healthy self-image among His people.

This procedure can be found in Acts 2:42–45, as follows:

"They devoted themselves to the apostles' teaching and to the fellowship, to the breaking of bread and to prayer. Everyone was filled with awe, and many wonders and miraculous signs were done by the apostles. All the believers were together and had everything in common. Selling their possessions and goods, they gave to anyone as he had need."

From the foregoing passage, we learn of three avenues of experience leading into God's plan in the early church:

1. Teaching was of vital importance. The body of Christ devoted themselves to the teachings of the apostles. Since the early church was basically made

up of Jewish believers, they were familiar with the Old Testament emphasis on teaching.

2. Also of importance was the fellowship and relational experience found in the breaking of bread and also in prayer. All the believers were together and had everything in common.

3. There was an emphasis on the experience of witnessing. Witnessing in the New Testament and early church consisted of seriously living the new Christian life and then talking about it. It was the selling of possessions and giving to those in need. What a sign that must have been to the nonbelievers!

These three elements make up God's reparenting process. This process is also known as "discipleship." In this true sense of reparenting, the entire body of Christ takes part and all are agents of growth for all.

Another part of this process is to read the Word of God. It is through God's Word that we learn of His attributes and character. It is through the Word of God that we receive "transformation of the mind." Then, it is through the body of

Christ that all becomes reality. It is through this analogy that the church, the body of Christ, is to demonstrate the character and attributes of God to all the people. Not all churches are performing this task, are they?

It is the organism we know as the church that is to be the avenue or roadway to freedom through the healing of a wounded self-image. It is one thing to "hear" God's message of unconditional love in the pastor's sermon, but when the love of Jesus flows into the wounded souls and hearts, we see the results of healing one's self-image. Those who experience it are set free to be.

Ponder Page

1. Are you still believing Satan's lies about you? Go back to the Five R's; rebuke and renounce these lies. (If you are a Christian, you *do* have the power and authority to do this!)

2. Go back to the characterization of God as suggested by J. B. Phillips. How do you perceive God? How do you relate to Him now?

3. Refocus on God's true character. Use these characteristics to replace any of your false images of God.

4. What is your self-image? Is this in line with the Word of God as to how He sees you?

5. Are you ready to escape the prison of what others may think of you?

6. What is your escape plan?

Chapter 4

The Steps to Change

Following are the steps that you are required to take if you wish for lasting change:

1. Change your self-image by submitting yourself to God's parenting process. Submission is step number one. This is sometimes the most difficult!

2. Pray. This is a necessity! It is through prayer that God will reveal what needs to be changed about your self-image. Ask Him to reveal the weakest area of your self-image.

3. Seek the Word of God. It is only through God's Word that you will know when and where transformation can take place.

4. Seek the body of Christ. Submit to the church as the body of Christ. Perhaps it needs to be mentioned that it is crucial that you seek and be in a healthy church. There are many dysfunctional churches in which a person

with a wounded self-image can actually be "destroyed." Some churches "shoot their wounded." Be careful! A healthy church will encourage not only God's peace, but also a sense of joy in the worship. Avoid churches where there is no joy. One of the characteristics and benefits of a healthy self-image is the ability to relax, have fun, and experience the joy of Jesus. It is okay to have a good time with our Lord. Did you know that? This will aid in physical and emotional healing, bringing about freedom and maturity.

5. Stay in a healthy church. It is here in this atmosphere that the process of healing through acceptance and unconditional love will take place. Remember that this is a process, and do not be too hard on yourself when transformation does not occur as fast as you think it should.

6. Make healthy choices. God has given us the freedom to make choices; use this freedom wisely. Holy Scripture is quite clear that even though God has given us free will (choice), He really beseeches us to "choose life." See Deuteronomy 30, beginning with verse 11: "Now

what I am commanding you today is not difficult for you or beyond your reach." Verses 19–20 further tell us, "This day I call heaven and earth as witnesses against you that I have set before you life and death, blessings and curses. Now choose life, so that you and your children may live and that you may love the Lord, listen to His voice, and hold fast to Him." We are free to be the divine original that God created us to be!

7. After taking the previous step, decide that you will no longer listen to Satan's lies, deceit, and/or accusations. Are you going to receive ideas about yourself from Satan or from God? It is that simple! Decide: "I will no longer listen to Satan's lies! I am going to listen to God and receive God's opinion of me as it is written. I will let my Lord reprogram my thoughts and feelings about myself."

8. As a continuation of step 7, become a partner with God in the reprogramming and renewal process. This continuing process will take place as you cooperate with the Holy Spirit. Any time you find yourself making an attempt to belittle yourself, ask God for His image of

you. Allow God's unconditional love to flow; allow God to lead you and teach you through His truth. The Holy Spirit will always lead you to God's truth!

9. Relax and enjoy God's creation as people with a healthy self-image do!

Habits to Learn to Help with Self-Image

Keep in your mind the word *process* and the word *progress*. You may sometimes hear the statement "Practice makes perfect." A more realistic statement may be "Through the process, progress is made." This journey is a progression of improvements to one's own image and corrections to one's image of God. It is also a process. Do not be too hard on yourself when God convicts you of the need to change your self-image. It took many years for you to develop the false image you have of yourself, so it may take some time for the renewal of your mind to take place. However, do not put your God in a box. Behave assertively but not aggressively. Behave assertively even when you do not feel like it.

When you fail, admit it and confess it to God. Then refuse to condemn yourself! Recite Romans 8:1, telling yourself, "There is now no condemnation for those who are in Christ Jesus." You are in the process of becoming like Jesus Christ. Growth takes time! Be kind to yourself during this process.

Do not compare yourself with others. Remember the David Icke quotation mentioned earlier: "The greatest prison people live in is the fear of what people think [of them]." You are a unique individual, and God enjoys your uniqueness. (*Note:* I recall times in my childhood when I allowed others to compare me to peers. I therefore would like to add the warning that you should not allow this to happen to you. I also was academically compared in school to my older sister. This was soon put an end to when my mother went to the school to advise that they stop the nonsense of comparing the two of us and start to recognize my sister and me as two different unique individuals!)

Concentrate and meditate on God's grace, unconditional love, and acceptance, and not upon criticisms of others. Associate with friends who are positive, who delight in who you are, and who also enjoy life. Start helping others to see themselves as God sees them, and encourage them. Give them the dignity afforded to God's unique creation. Learn to laugh!

Look for the humor in life and experience it. Learn to be free to laugh at yourself as well. Do not take life so seriously! Sometimes we can take life "responsibly" and still not be too serious about it. If you have expectations of others, make sure those expectations are realistic.

Learn to relax and take life easy. Again, you can do this and still approach life with a sense of responsibility. Remember, God prepared Jesus for a period spanning more than thirty years before His three years of ministry. Let's not get ahead of God.

Do what is right and pleasing in the eyes of God. When our lives reflect God's character, we are a lot happier—and this affects our attitude about ourselves.

Be positive in your life. Try to avoid being negative about other people or situations.

Lead other people with your influence and guidance rather than with autocratic power.

Love according to God's model of agape love, and balance love with limits.

Always remember, silence is okay and even required at times! Too many of us believe there always has to be conversation going on, even when we are in prayer. When I used to teach about prayer, I always emphasized that the greatest part of prayer is listening to God's response in the silence. Noise can blot out what God may be trying to communicate to you. I do not recall where I read this, but I have never forgotten it: "Only those who care about you can hear you when you're quiet." Silence is (can be) golden. About sixty years ago, I purchased the book *In the Stillness Is the Dancing*. I still believe this today—and I am still dancing!

To sum up these suggestions, I refer to the apostle Paul's words in Colossians 3:13b, 3:14–17:

> Forgive as the Lord forgave you. And over all these virtues put on love which binds them all together in perfect unity. Let the peace of Christ rule in your hearts, since as members of one body you were called to peace. And be thankful. Let the word of Christ dwell in you richly as you teach and admonish one another with all wisdom, and as you sing psalms, hymns, and spiritual songs with gratitude in your hearts to God. And whatever you do, whether in word or deed, do it all in the name of our Lord Jesus, giving thanks to God the Father through Him.

To review, as your self-image is brought into balance with God's image of you, you are then able to pursue your freedom to be. You are no longer in the bondage of Satan's snare! However, the battle of the mind will continue. You'll constantly need to ward off the lies of the accuser of the brethren. You'll also need to remain humble throughout the process!

You need to continue the battle for the control of your mind. The next chapter will deal with this continual struggle of the renewing of the mind. It is not easy! However, it is scriptural.

Ponder Page

1. What will you do to intensify your searching what God's Word has to say about you? The more you read His Word, the more you will begin to see yourself as God sees you.

2. Do you still compare yourself to others? Are you concerned about what others think of you? If so, stop this by asking for God's help and refocusing on what His Word has to say about you.

3. Begin to see an image of God as being your cheerleader!

4. "In the silence is the dancing." Do you have a problem seeking silence? It is in the silence that God desires to talk to you.

Chapter 5

Our Freedom Fighters (God's Secret Weapon)

Our freedom fighters are more than just friends, although they might be considered as our friends. This is a much deeper relationship, as well as a need. A freedom fighter will have a positive attitude and will share the same thoughts and goals of the person he or she is supporting. The person will also be an inspirer, a motivator, a faith builder, and one who expresses unconditional love. I personally focus on Ephesians 6:10–11, "to be strong in the Lord and his mighty power. Put on all of God's armor so that you [I] will be able to stand firm against all strategies of the devil." In other words, my freedom fighter is also my armor-bearer, one who spiritually helps me put on my armor every morning.

Those who seek to be set free to be need this type of support to keep them on track and encouraged with compassion, hope, unconditional love, and accountability, especially when the enemy tries to intervene and pull them away from their godly mission, which is to be set free of Satan's whims and journey into freedom. Go through your own list of potential freedom fighters you can call upon. Ask for guidance from the Holy Spirit. Ask that He direct you and give you wisdom directly from Him to get started. Who will be your freedom fighters?

These can be people from the present. However, I chose some people from my past whom I could count on. Some of these people kept me on God's path years ago. In any event, freedom fighters are any people you have witnessed in your life, or even fictional characters you have read about, who will stand in the gap for you at any time. Some of those on my list are people I have never met and probably never will meet. They are names I can call upon, even if only in my thoughts, to get myself back on track.

The following is a partial list, in near to chronological order, of my freedom fighters, just to give you some ideas for people from your past you might select:

My Mom and Dad

No, my parents were not perfect. Neither was I! I did grow up in the midst of the Great Depression, and we learned how to get along without such items as automobiles for transportation—and no bikes for me and my two siblings. There were also no meals in restaurants for us. We learned how to better utilize utilities such as water and electricity, how to save on clothing (Mom would knit our sweaters, which she would rip and reknit when we outgrew them), etc. You get the picture? On top of this, my dad was crippled with arthritis as far back as I can remember. It started with him walking with a limp and in pain because his knee was "frozen" or locked. Then I witnessed him using crutches, and then he used a wheelchair later in his journey. I am sure he missed playing baseball, playing catch, and doing other activities with his kids. I remember stories of his doctor telling him he needed to be confined to bed; his reply was that he had a family to feed, clothe, and shelter and could not quit! Dad had the attitude that in life, you play the hand that God deals you and make the most of it.

Dad was an incredible nurturer toward me even though we never had the opportunity to play catch or go to ball games together. He was always looking out for me as I went to Scout meetings. He became a member of the Saint Louis Council of the Boy Scouts and also attended PTA meetings with my mom. It was a painful loss for me when he departed this world much too soon at the age of fifty-two. The pain remains to this day. Yes, more than six decades later, I still miss him. As I look back on his short life full of love for his family, I honestly believe my dad lived free to be and gave me glimpses of kingdom living in spite of his situation.

My small four-foot, eleven-inch mom took care of him. She weighed under two pounds when born out in the country in Missouri, where for her first winter she survived by being placed in a cigar box set on the oven door in the kitchen. Her mom dressed her in doll clothes. She was always a fighter for survival and outlived her six siblings! I loved Mom and Dad's sacrifices for us, and I learned so much about life just by being in their presence.

When I started first grade, my teacher was the woman who had taught my older sister when she was in first grade. I was constantly being criticized, until my little mom came into our classroom one afternoon and read the riot act to the teacher. She announced that as long as I was doing the best work I could do, she would be pleased with all my grades and insisted that I not be compared to my sister anymore in terms of our grades.

I still have this picture in my mind; it pops into view whenever someone is comparing me to someone else. Thanks, Mom!

She always had the heart of a servant. Sometime after my dad's death, Mom began a ministry for blind women. She would pick up several of them at their homes and drive them around various parts of Saint Louis. She became their eyes and would describe what she was seeing to them. My servanthood developed through watching her minister to others. I certainly learned through my parents that all is possible through God and that I, too, would play the hand that God had dealt to me!

Greg Toole

Greg has been my prayer partner and accountability partner for the last several years. When I was living in Jacksonville, Florida, he and I would meet for breakfast every Monday morning. (For those of you reading *Free to Be* from the southern USA, we did have cheese grits on Monday!) This was a Holy Spirit event in both our lives (not the cheese grits!) and was always followed by great prayer time together. We made an agreement that through the internet and FaceTime, we would continue to meet in prayer, accountability, and thanksgiving every Monday morning. Our time together usually flows for a couple of hours. Greg has been an inspiration as God put the pages together for *Free to Be*. During our prayer time, and even in the silence, God would bring forth something that He would inspire me to include here. Greg and I look forward to our Mondays together as God continues to anoint him with discernment and wisdom and allows us both to be free to be. Greg is my weekly freedom fighter. I feel the presence of his prayers during the week as well.

Charles A. Lindbergh

This one probably sounds a bit strange! My respect for Charles Lindbergh goes way back to my preteen years. As mentioned earlier, my mom did a great job reading to me as a child and developed my early reading habits. I remember when the public library opened in our suburban Saint Louis community and how I thrived on reading nonfiction books. One of my favorites in the early 1930s, when I was ten or eleven years old, was Charles Lindbergh's autobiographical account of his solo flight across the Atlantic Ocean from New York to Paris, France, in a single-engine plane. He started as an unknown twenty-five-year-old mail pilot and became the most famous person in the world at that time! His book title was *We*. The flight's first problem was the departure from a muddy tarmac. Lindbergh's personal struggles came later. He was an overcomer, fighting unknown hazards along the way. Obviously, he became a victorious overcomer of a type that we all strive to be. To fight off fatigue, he even attempted flying so close to the surface of the ocean as to get a cold ocean spray upon his face. He fought off icing of the wings on his *Spirit of St. Louis* airplane. And then came more fatigue. And storms over the huge ocean.

Why did this person I had never met become one of my freedom fighters? Whenever I'm dealing with unknown storms, fatigue, or my own what-ifs, I relate to the adventurous events of Charles A. Lindbergh's journey into his unknown. He had the tenacity and faith to deal with his issues and received an extra dose of perseverance from "somewhere." He claimed, "I can do it," and I claim my own "I can do it" as expressed in Philippians 4:13: "I can do everything through Christ who gives me strength." Lindbergh was asked why the title of his autobiography was *We*. His response was to refer to the spiritual partnership between man and airplane. My "We" is the bond or partnership between man (me) and Jesus, in whom I place my faith.

Mohandas Gandhi

At least fifty years ago, I had a large poster of Mohandas Gandhi hanging on my office wall. I think it was issued by an insurance company at that time. Underneath his huge portrait were the following words: "In a Gentle Way You Can Change the World." Keep in mind that in the 1960s, there was a rebellion of young people who were upset and protested the Vietnam War. At the time, I thought, *what a great revelation and a great reason to offer to end the unrest and protests!* Gandhi preached nonviolence and freedom with attempts to inspire leaders across the world. His words were "Where there is love, there is life."

I was intrigued, desiring to learn more of this man from halfway across the globe. I began reading a few of his biographies. *Gandhi, a Hindu* tells the story of an event in

Gandhi's young life when he was living in England as a student. One Sunday afternoon, he recalled, there was a knock at his door. Lo and behold, the young man in the hallway was a Bible salesman! Although Gandhi was not interested in his product, the sales pitch was overwhelming for him. In order to terminate this onslaught, Gandhi reached into his pocket for enough money to purchase the wares and get rid of his unwelcome intruder. When peace finally settled back in, he began to skim through this newly purchased book. He was led by God to open chapters 5, 6, and 7 of the Gospel of Matthew. The more he read, the more he was mesmerized by the writings. By late afternoon, Gandhi confessed that if it weren't for what the "Western world" had done to misinterpret the writings, he would have become a Christian that afternoon. The writings of God in the beatitudes were what led him to become a man who believed and acted out the idea that in a gentle way, you can change the world.

This story still strengthens my belief that we never know who we'll touch with Jesus in our own lives as we journey through our time on earth. There are times when God desires no more from us than to plant some seeds of faith and hope into strangers. Others will come behind to water or fertilize those planted seeds, and still others will witness the harvest! All working for the glory of God.

As you read about this "small" event in Gandhi's life, reflect on how this unknown (to us, but not to God) Bible salesman impacted Gandhi, who in turn changed the world. He was used by God as a seed planter!

Some of the aforementioned people are ones who have followed along with me as freedom fighters. And I am grateful for each one of them! An important PS to this story is that the love never dies. The story of Mohandas Gandhi is what inspired Martin Luther King on his godly journey to change the world in a gentle way. And on it goes, forever.

General George S. Patton

I include General Patton as another of my freedom fighters as he was fighting for our nation and world during World War II. I know about him from my teenage years in the 1940s and by reading Bill O'Reilly's book *Killing Patton*. To begin my reasoning, I believe Patton had a prophetic message about Russia's being a potential threat rather than an ally. His attitude was focused upon victory and total defeat of his enemy, similar to our attitude of defeating our enemy, Satan. When given tasks that seemed impossible to others, Patton saw them as an opportunity for possibilities and believed that miracles would happen. He believed in himself. Military doctrine said it was impossible to do what was being asked of General Patton. His mind focused upon *I can do it!* General Patton also trained his troops to follow him into victory.

By focusing on my attitude as General Patton focused on his, I, too, can conquer those negative thoughts if and when they enter my mind. "God, you and I can do this together!"

The Man of La Mancha

Uh-oh! Before you begin comparing me with the hero of *The Man of La Mancha* and declare me as looney as he was, hear me out! I assure you, reader, that I will *not* be fighting and chasing after windmills as the man did in the play. However, I confess I am chasing after impossible dreams

The Man of La Mancha sees the heroine, Aldonza, not as the street urchin prostitute that she is; he sees the godly beauty in her. She does not accept his vision of her and remains focused on her image as a tramp until the end, when she accepts her beauty and becomes Dulcinea, the name he gives her. I share this with you only because of the anointing God gave my wife Anne and me to witness to God's love to the unaffirmed, hurting people in this world. Yes, we have witnessed God turning many Aldonzas into Dulcineas.

I also seem haunted by the lyrics of the song sung by the Man of La Mancha as it pertains to the quest God has given me. It is also a reminder from my freedom fighter, this fictional character I first "met" years ago, never to get off track. When Jesus entered into my life, my impossible dream became possible! Now, I can do all things through Him who strengthens and directs me. I also found myself fighting a beatable foe, namely, the evil forces in the world today. As I have ministered with so many over these forty-plus years, I also found my arms (body, emotions, and mind) too weary. However, to reach for that star of possibilities is not a hopeless endeavor! When I zero in on Romans 15:13, "I pray that God, the source of hope, will fill you [and me] completely with joy and peace because you [we] trust in him. Then [we] will overflow with confident hope through the power of the Holy Spirit." Hopelessness disappears! With my God, I will march into hell for a heavenly cause to witness the captives set free, and then my heart, where Jesus resides, "will be peaceful and calm when I'm laid to my rest." When I think of "the world will be better for this," I remember my Boy Scout camping days. I was always taught to leave our campsite in better shape than when we first arrived. This has always stuck in my mind, and it is *only* through God that I can leave this temporary home in better shape than when I arrived. This is my quest to reach that unreachable star. Thanks be to God for bringing the Man of La Mancha into my life as one of my freedom fighters to guide me to His reachable star.

Pastor Dietrich Bonhoeffer

Hopefully, this is not another uh-oh like the previous freedom fighter. Dietrich Bonhoeffer was martyred for his beliefs near the conclusion of World War II as he opposed Nazism and was part of a plot to assassinate Adolf Hitler and stage a coup. Not many people are seeking the gift of martyrdom, including me! There have been many books written and movies made on the life and death of this famous freedom fighter from Germany. I will make no attempt to write another! I suggest if you are unfamiliar with this name, you should check into Bonhoeffer on the internet. You will get inundated with good reading material, hopefully.

I first became mesmerized by Bonhoeffer's commitment to true sacrificial living in the mid-1960s during my early walk with Jesus. It was by reading several of his well-known books that I learned what it means to live in freedom, discipleship, and responsibility. Bonhoeffer knew what it meant to be totally free and totally surrendered to the living God.

The following are several quotations on freedom from Bonhoeffer's book *Letters and Papers from Prison*.

He lists his four "stations on the road to freedom," as follows:

1. Discipline

   "Only through discipline may a man learn to be free."

2. Action

   "Freedom comes only through deeds, not through thoughts taking wing."

3. Suffering

   "Only for one blissful moment could you draw near to touch freedom; then, it might be perfected in glory, you gave it to God."

4. Death

   "Freedom, how long we have sought thee in discipline, action, and suffering; dying, we now may behold thee revealed in the Lord."

   This reminds me of the call from Jesus to "die to self-daily."

5. Bonhoeffer's concern for the local church is evident in his statement, "I wonder whether it is possible (it almost seems so today) to regain the idea of the church as providing an understanding of the area of freedom."

Zorba the Greek

This small book, *Free to Be*, opened with the story of Zorba entering my life. Now as this approaches completion, I take you back to Zorba once again.

Because I relate to Zorba as one of my top go-to guys,

it really is a toss-up for me to classify him as a fictional or nonfictional character. You may need to decide. After I share a bit, hopefully you will understand why I have difficulty with how to classify him. It is also difficult to separate Zorba from Nikos Kazantzakis, the author of *Zorba the Greek*, and even Anthony Quinn, who played the role of Zorba in the movie and Broadway play presentation! This needs an explanation.

First, you will need to go back to the beginning of *Free to Be* to rediscover how the movie *Zorba the Greek* impacted my life and brought me into a relationship with Jesus. Then, probably in the early 1980s, the Broadway production of *Zorba* was scheduled to arrive in Louisville. I wrote a personal letter to Anthony Quinn explaining my conversion and how Zorba had played a part in this. In the letter, I wrote, "God the Father created me to dance; God the Son gave me permission to dance; God the Holy Spirit, through Zorba, taught me to dance." (You need to see the movie to know the significance of dancing.) I even invited Quinn to our home for dinner!

I was surprised and pleased to get a response from him and even an explanation that he needed to decline the dinner invitation what with rehearsals et cetera. However, he did want to meet me and my wife Anne after the conclusion of the performance.

At intermission, we were approached by an usher, who announced she was to take us backstage just before the curtain call for Mr. Quinn. It was an honor to meet him in his dressing room at the conclusion of the show. I was surprised at his size. Upon reading his autobiography, I learned he had been a professional boxer before his movie career. We both shared touching stories of how Zorba had impacted both our lives, and he explained how he felt to have become Zorba. It seemed neither one of us wanted to end the time of sharing.

As Anne and I were leaving, Anthony (Tony) Quinn gave me a huge and a tight bear hug, and softly said to me three times, "God bless you, my son." He began to weep, I began to weep. Anne was teary, and so was his secretary, who was in the room with us. Zorba had truly made an impact on him and also on me. Anthony shared with us how much knowing—and being—Zorba had changed his attitude toward life.

I have also learned that my friend Zorba made an impact on the English poet and playwright Christopher Fry. Fry begins his touching poem "Christmas Faith" as follows:

Celebration is to greet life with a shout of "Yes!"
instead of a "Maybe"; to dance like Zorba the Greek,
out of exuberance of our indebtedness to sing out the
joy of our appreciation!

Then there are the unusual comments from the author of the book *Zorba the Greek*, Niko Kazantzakis, who claimed how much the enthusiasm of his creation Zorba continued to haunt him! Kazantzakis was quoted as saying, "I hope nothing. I fear nothing. I am free!" That freedom overflowed into his creation of Zorba. During the entire production, you can feel the conflict between the freedom of Zorba and the imprisonment and stuffiness of his English friend. From my recollection, the Englishman read books *about* life, whereas Zorba *lived* life—to the fullest! He summed this up with the following words to his friend: "You have everything but one thing: madness. A man needs a little madness, or else he never dares cut the rope to be free!" When my friend Zorba says this, I suggest you focus upon our need to care more about life itself and less about what others think of you. In the long run of life, not even death can harm us. When we reach the mindset of fearing nothing, like Zorba, we will achieve the freedom that God is aching for us to receive and exuberate! And, like Zorba, we will dance free with Jesus. Free to be! Yes, our freedom to be comes when we cut the rope and become the person God calls us to be, rather than the one we or others think we should be.

Now to my final freedom fighter, God's Word through Yeshua Ha Mashiach—Jesus our Messiah.

I conclude this phase of my journey with Zorba, my dance instructor, with a poem I read almost forty years ago that still haunts me. The title is "Give Me Madness," written by Sam Keen and published in his book *To a Dancing God* (how appropriate for Zorba!).

> God, I want to surrender to the rhythm of music and sea,
> To the seasons of ebb and flow, to the tidal surge of love.
>
> I am tired of being hard, tight, controlled, tensed against tenderness, afraid of softness.
> I am tired of directing my world, making, doing, shaping.
>
> Tension is ecstasy in chains. The muscles are tightened to prevent trembling.
> Nerves strained to prevent trust. Hope, relaxation.
>
> Surrender is a risk no sane man may take. Sanity never surrendered is a burden no man may carry.

God, give me madness that does not destroy wisdom, responsibility, love."

Jesus Our Messiah, the Word of God

There are many scriptures mentioned throughout *Free to Be*. I'll give you a few more that help me when I hear God's call upon my life into freedom with Him. A few worth repeating and worthy of hanging on to are as follows:

- Psalm 118:6

  The Lord is for me, so I will have *no* fear. What can mere people do to me?

- Psalm 144:1–2

  Praise the Lord, who is my Rock. He trains my hands for war and gives my fingers skill for battle. He is my loving ally and my fortress, my tower of safety, my rescuer.

- Proverbs 29:25

  Fearing people is a dangerous trap, but trusting the Lord means safety.

- John 8:32, 8:36

  And you will know the truth, and the truth *will* set you free. … So, if the Son sets you free, you *are* truly free.

- Romans 6:18, 6:22

  Now you *are* free from your slavery to sin, and you have become slaves to righteous living. … But now you are *free* from the power of sin and have become slaves of God.

- 1 Corinthians 16:13–14

  Be on guard. Stand firm in the faith. *Be* courageous. *Be* strong. And do everything with *love*.

- 2 Corinthians 3:17

  For the Lord *is* the Spirit, and wherever the Spirit of the Lord is, there *is* freedom.

- Colossians 1:13–14

  For He has rescued us from the kingdom of darkness and transferred us into the kingdom of his dear Son, who *purchased* our *freedom* and forgave our sins.

- 1 John 4:1

  Dear friends, do not believe everyone who claims to speak by the Spirit. You must test them to see if the spirit they have comes from God.

  (*Note:* For the foregoing quotations, all italics are mine, for emphasis.)

Please memorize your own verses dealing with God's call upon your life to march into freedom with him for a wonderful cause: your freedom in your journey with him! Never lose hope in your journey. Learn to dance with God as Zorba has taught us. You and Jesus make up your own dance routines. Have fun! He desires to rejoice with you, and you with Him! I leave you with Paul's prayer of hope as found in Romans 15:13:

> I pray that God, the source of hope, will fill you completely with joy and peace because you trust in Him. Then you will overflow with confident hope through the power of the Holy Spirit. In the mighty name of Jesus, our Messiah, the One who walks and talks with us as we journey into freedom with him. Amen.

Ponder Page

1. Reread Bonhoeffer's "Four Stations on the Road to Freedom." Where do you see yourself on this road?

2. Who will be your freedom fighters? Begin your list and contact a few willing to participate on your behalf.

3. To "die to self" doesn't come easily. However, the more often you do this, the more it will flow into your journey into freedom. Can you trust in God? Will you begin to trust God today?

4. Do your hopes and dreams still feel impossible to achieve, even with the Holy Spirit whispering into your ears, "All is possible with Me"?

5. Who is your "dance instructor"? Will you accept Jesus's invitation to dance with Him?

6. Always focus upon *the best, which is yet to come*!

Afterword

By The Rt. Rev. Carl E. Buffington, Jr.

Don Bloch talks about his freedom fighters in chapter 5 of this book, *Free to Be*. When I saw the title, I immediately thought of the communion of saints. And as I read *Free to Be*, I thought of saints and heroes: models of morality or mirrors of identity?

One freedom fighter who came to my mind was Mel Gibson as William Wallace in *Braveheart*, at least in terms of the word *freedom* being used. There are a couple of places where *freedom* just jumps off the screen. One is where Wallace is leading his men into battle while he talks about death as not being as much of a matter of consequence as it is a matter of freedom. The other is where Wallace has been disemboweled and will momentarily be decapitated, and he manages to somehow, beyond human strength, pull up and shout out *freedom* one last time. Freedom mattered to William Wallace.

Freedom matters! And there is greater freedom that matters more than the type depicted in the movie. Because this freedom frees us from sin and death, and opens the door to life abundant in the here and now, and to life eternal in the now and not yet. That's freedom! And it, too, was worth dying for, with a much greater benefit for us all.

As Don points out, the problem of not being free began a long time ago, in the Garden, with an issue of disobedience. And it's no minor problem. There was a price to be paid for our freedom, one that all of us collectively couldn't bankroll. It would take God to intervene. God would have to do something, and He would do something, over and over again.

At one time in history God raised up a savior for his people, Moses, a freedom fighter of the highest order. He would set his people free from slavery in Egypt. The story would almost obnoxiously be repeated over and over again in the book of Judges. God would raise up a deliverer and more freedom fighters; He would be successful; and the people would be set free. That is, until they started sinning all over again. What wasn't working?

And then one day God, in the flesh, appeared. And God in the flesh said that the truth would set us free. He went on to say that He was the truth, "I am the way, the truth, and the life." Jesus came, having been sent with the mission to set us free.

Don talks about people who have lived free, freedom fighters such as Bonhoeffer who said things like, "Obedience without freedom is slavery. Freedom without obedience is arbitrary self-will." And I remember, sort of well, the gist of the words of Bishop Bill Frey of Colorado, who compared his new life in Jesus to falling out of a plane at thirty thousand feet. "Splat! I was dead, really dead, and then I got up. I was alive. Alive in Jesus! And I realized I had no fear. What could anyone do to me? hold over me? threaten me with? I was free. I am free!" Christ was alive in him, and he was alive in Christ.

I used to walk the French Quarter with one of my freedom fighter friends, Brennan Manning, stopping at one gelato bar after another. He had a saying, "Love God and do as you please." Most people tend to equate freedom with doing whatever they want to do—the second bit of the sentence.

But freedom is found in doing and being what we are created to be and to do. God knit us together in our mother's womb, the psalmist tells us, and called us into being with a plan and purpose—His will. It's like doing what we were made for, becoming who we were made to be. Like a fish is to water. And as we move more and more into that becoming, we experience more and more of His love consequently, and more and more of our freedom.

So, the key to Brennan's axiom is found in the first two words, "Love God." In loving Him, we will want to do His will. In desiring His will, we begin to do His will, which is where we find not only freedom but also fulfillment of living, life. It's in realizing who we are as His beloved that we find freedom— freedom to do, freedom to be.

There are so many bumps along the road to freedom, some internal and some external. We need our freedom fighters from today and from ages past. The good news of this brief book *Free to Be* is that packed into it are some really helpful and very practical ways for us to navigate our way to freedom.

There's a phrase in this Collect of Peace from the Morning Prayer Service in the Book of Common Prayer that has always stuck with me. At first it sounds almost oxymoronic, equating service with perfect freedom. But I remember once hearing, another of my freedom fighters, Dallas Willard, say something similar to, 'When we are totally surrendered to His will and service, then we are free to do whatever we want."

> O God, who art the author of peace and lover of concord, in knowledge of whom standeth our eternal life, *whose service is perfect freedom*: Defend us, thy humble servants, in all assaults of our enemies; that we, surely trusting in thy defense, may not fear the power of any adversaries; through the might of Jesus Christ our Lord. Amen.

Acknowledgments

A special thanks for the encouragement and help I received along this journey into going solo writing *Free to Be*.

Thanks to Joye Cassady for her expertise in setting up my computer to do its stuff to document this endeavor. Even being eight hundred miles away, she was able to set up the laptop and get the ball rolling. She was always there when help was needed!

Thanks to my wife Anne, who was—and still is—commander in chief of encouragement. She was always there when I needed a pick-me-up when I felt stuck. She also was a great original proofreader for me.

As mentioned within the pages of *Free to Be*, Greg Toole was always on hand, especially for our Monday morning FaceTime meetings, to meet my needs of encouragement along this journey.

Thanks to my advisor and guide at Archway Publishing, Deena Capron. She was always there when I hit a temporary "road block." Her wisdom and compassion got me through what appeared to me as a stumbling block.

A special thank-you to my special and beloved mentors along the journey, Francis and Judith MacNutt and Dennis and Rita Bennett. Their wisdom was priceless to me as I absorbed as much as possible their dedication to each other and their love for the King of kings.

Bibliography

Anderson, Neil. *The Bondage Breaker.* Eugene: Harvest House, 2007.

Backus, William, and Marie Chapian. *Telling Yourself the Truth.* Minneapolis: Bethany House, 1994.

Bunyan, John (rewritten by Mary Godolphin). *Pilgrim's Progress.* New York: J. B. Lippincott, 1934.

Bonhoeffer, Dietrich. *Letters and Papers from Prison.* New York: Macmillan, 1953.

Cloud, Henry. *Changes that Heal.* Grand Rapids, MI: Zondervan, 1990.

Eden's Bridge. "I Will Change Your Name." *Celtic Worship,* vol. 2, 1998.

MacNutt, Francis. *Healing.* Notre Dame, IN: Ave Maria, 1974.

———. *Deliverance from Evil Spirits.* Grand Rapids, MI. Chosen Books. 1995.

McDowell, Josh. *His Image, My Image.* Nashville, TN: Thomas Nelson, 1984.

O'Reilly, Bill, and Martin Dugard. *Killing Patton.* New York: Henry Holt & Company, 2014.

Phillips, J. B. *Your God Is Too Small.* New York: Macmillan, 1961.

Sandford, John, and Paula Sandford. *The Transformation of the Inner Man.* South Plainfield, NJ: Bridge, 1982.

Schlink, Basilea. *My All for Him.* Darmstadt, Germany: Evangelical Sisterhood of Mary, 2017.

Seamands, David A. *Healing for Damaged Emotions.* Wheaton, IL. Victor Books, 1989.

Swindoll, Charles R. *The Grace Awakening.* New York: Walker & Co., 1990.

Wagner, Doris M. *How to Minister Freedom.* Minneapolis: Chosen Books, 2005.

Wagner, Maurice E. The *Sensation of Being Somebody.* Grand Rapids, MI: Zondervan, 1975.

White, Thomas B. *The Believer's Guide to Spiritual Warfare.* Ann Arbor: Vine Books, 1990.

Wright, Alan D. *Free Yourself, Be Yourself.* Colorado Springs: Multnomah Books, 2010.

CPSIA information can be obtained
at www.ICGtesting.com
Printed in the USA
BVHW031935200422
634706BV00028B/134